LITERACY EVALUATION

Issues & Practicalities

edited by

Chrystine Bouffler

Heinemann
Portsmouth, NH

Primary English Teaching Association
NSW, Australia

Heinemann
A division of Reed Publishing (USA), Inc.
361 Hanover Street, Portsmouth, NH 03801-3912
Offices and agents throughout the world

©1992 Primary English Teaching Association
Laura Street, Newtown NSW 2042 Australia

First U.S. Printing 1993
ISBN 0-435-08791-6 (Heinemann)

Library of Congress Cataloging-in-Publication Data

Literacy Evaluation: issues & practicalities / edited by Chrystine Bouffler.
   p. cm.
   Includes bibliographical references.
   ISBN 0-435-08791-6 (alk. paper)
   1. Language arts—Ability testing. 2. Reading—Ability testing.
3. Literacy. I. Bouffler, Chrystine.
LB1576.L553 1993b
372.6'044—dc20

92-44319
CIP

Cover design by Tony O'Connell
Designed by Tony O'Connell and Jeremy Steele
Edited by Jeremy Steele
Typeset in 11/13 Garamond at the HRD Centre
The Boulevarde and Toothill Street, Lewisham NSW 2049

Printed in the United States of America on Acid Free Paper
93 94 95 96 97 9 8 7 6 5 4 3 2 1

Contents

Notes on Contributors

Wendy Crebbin taught in many settings, mainly amongst 'difficult learners', before moving into teacher education. She currently lectures at both Ballarat University College and Deakin University.

Kaye Lowe, an experienced primary teacher, is now a lecturer in English at the University of Western Sydney, Nepean. Her interests include qualitative research, evaluation and parent education. *Bill Bintz* has had extensive experience of teaching English at secondary and tertiary levels and is completing a doctoral thesis on curriculum change in the primary school at Indiana University.

Penny Freppon is Director of the Manney Literacy Center at the University of Cincinnati.

John Dwyer is Executive Director, Review and Evaluation, with the Queensland Department of Education. He has long had an interest in language teaching and learning and edited *A Sea of Talk* for PETA in 1989.

Lexie Mincham has worked in the ESL field since 1974 — as a teacher, manager of an intensive language centre, consultant and, currently, curriculum officer responsible for assessment and evaluation.

Myra Barrs is Director of the Centre for Language in Primary Education in London. She played a leading role in the development of the Primary Language Record.

Vivienne Hayward is Principal Education Officer, English, with the Northern Territory Department of Education. Previously, over a twenty-two year period, she taught in England, Papua New Guinea, Kiribati and Australia.

Jan Hancock is a lecturer in education at Wollongong University, specialising in literacy education. Thirteen years in schools in various capacities have given her a strong interest in developing practical approaches to the evaluation of literacy development.

Roslyn Fryar, Nanette Johnston and *Jane Leaker* have worked as LLIMY (Literacy and Learning in the Middle Years) tutors in South Australia for the past three years. All hold co-ordinator positions in their present schools in conjunction with their classroom responsibilities.

Heather Fehring has been lecturing and publishing in the field of children's language development for fifteen years. Readers will know her best for her work on children's spelling and for her publications in the area of assessment and language profile development.

INTRODUCTION

Chrystine Bouffler

During a recent conversation a colleague remarked, 'Has there ever been a time when the teaching of language was not controversial?' Given the political nature of literacy, the answer is almost certainly no, but in this instance my colleague was referring to the changes and debates that have marked the last twenty-five years of literacy education. In the '70s it was the issues of how we read, how we learn to read and how children should be taught to read. During the '80s writing was in the spotlight. The work of Donald Graves and later the systemic linguists ensured that debates about the teaching of writing would provide grist for the educational mill. Assessment and evaluation are already shaping up as the issue of the '90s. However, it is an issue set in a very different political and economic climate, and whether it will be as passionately debated in educational circles remains to be seen. It certainly deserves more open discussion than it is currently getting.

Putting this book together has been very much a learning experience for me. Contributors to the book, and to my learning, are first and foremost reflective teachers. Some have other jobs or other roles as consultants, tutors, education officers or researchers. All, from their particular perspectives, have focused and clarified issues. Some of these issues are theoretical and go right to the heart of all education and all educational assessment. Others relate to overseas experience and what we can learn from it — still others to how teachers manage assessment in their classrooms. While each in its own way challenges traditional beliefs or practice, all must be seen within the context of social, economic and political developments both here and overseas.

The terms *assessment* and *evaluation* are often used interchangeably. Strictly speaking, assessment is the process by which information is gathered, and evaluation is the process of interpreting that information. You will find that the various writers have used either one or other, or both terms. However, they are so closely linked that you can scarcely have one without the other. At the risk of offending the purists, I have left the terms as the individual writers used them.

The debates associated with assessment differ somewhat from those that have surrounded reading and writing because they are and will continue to be argued within the framework of a more overt political agenda. To put it simply, governments have a greater stake in assessment than they had in previous debates, and their interest has been sharpened by the present economic climate. That is why there is an urgent need for teachers to become familiar with issues beyond those that pertain immediately to the classroom. Accordingly the aim of this book is to prompt informed debate, as well as to provide some examples of how teachers are dealing with assessment in their classrooms.

To understand current developments in assessment, it is necessary to understand how the world of work has changed in the last ten or fifteen years, and what this has meant for education. Where once we had only a small percentage of the work force in professional and semi-professional employment, with the rest in trades and unskilled or semi-skilled jobs, we now have a large increase in the number of professions and the people in them, with a marked decline in the number of skilled or semi-skilled jobs as technology takes over in this sector. In short, there has been a pronounced upward shift in the overall job profile. People who would have been office workers and tradespeople ten to fifteen years ago are now teachers, nurses, engineers, computer experts and so on.

This has had a number of consequences for education. The most obvious is that students are staying on at school longer and need to attain higher levels of literacy and numeracy. A less obvious consequence is the public perception that standards have declined and that schools are failing. It is not difficult to see how such a perception has developed. Let us assume that the general distribution of ability among the population is much the same in 1990 as it was in 1970. If we also assume for argument's sake that 10% of the population went to universities in 1970, and 20% in 1990 (the figures are hypothetical), we can agree it is inherently unlikely that the 10–20% will be just as able as the 0–10%. What is happening is that people are comparing different sections of the population and inferring that standards have declined because many of the students at universities today are not as good as they were in 1970. This kind of argument is being repeated in other walks of life. Administrators seeking to employ office staff are fishing in a different pool today, yet they blame schools because those they have to choose from do not possess the abilities of office workers of the '70s. There is no doubt that we need to look closely at what is going on in schools, but it is unfair to criticise educators for what is beyond their control.

The perception of declining standards has been coupled with a decline in employment as a result of the depression. Money is tight and governments feel more accountable for their spending. They want better educational value for the dollars spent on education. They want to know that standards are improving, which means assessing the performance of their education systems. There have been other significant factors in the push for system-wide assessment (not least the emerging climate of economic rationalism), but it is not my intention to pursue them here — except to say that the push for accountability and assessment is world-wide, as a number of the following chapters will demonstrate.

Assessment is an integral part of teaching. Although there is no doubt that teachers are best placed to make judgements about children's learning, in the past they have commonly relied on standardised forms of assessment. Indeed, in circumstances where they needed to report to the system or to parents, they often had very little choice. Now, however, the expertise of teachers in making judgements has been recognised in alternate forms of assessment, which are presently being mandated. This move away from standardised testing to a system of profiling is potentially a very positive development, providing that teachers are informed about the issues and have developed a thorough understanding of language and literacy.

I believe it is vital that teachers control the use of profiles: otherwise the profiles will control what is taught. In NSW external tests are used as a means of gathering information about the system, and this is already affecting what is taught in classrooms. There is a danger that profiling will turn out to be little different in this regard. Many, particularly politicians, believe that would not be a bad thing. They have a view of knowledge and learning which Crebbin describes as a consumption view, and Lowe & Bintz refer to as a transmission model. However, teachers who wish to see children in charge of their own learning, and themselves as facilitators and supporters of that learning, are likely to have a different view of knowledge and of assessment.

While nobody would deny that governments and systems have a legitimate right to assess — indeed Dwyer argues that there are very good reasons why they should do so — the question is whether the same form of assessment can satisfy the needs of all groups. Dwyer and Mincham both believe that profiling has the potential to provide information to the individual teacher *and* to the system. On the other hand, Lowe & Bintz argue that the search for a single evaluation model is futile, since those concerned have different views of knowledge, literacy and learning and require different kinds of information. In a complementary case study, Freppon describes the situation of a teacher trying to reconcile her own assessment needs and the divergent demands of her school system.

Governments and systems need aggregated information. They are concerned with the overall picture, not with individuals. The process of gathering the necessary information must be cost-effective, and it must allow for comparisons to be made from year to year if improvements are to be demonstrated. It is in this process of aggregation and the likely development of national standards that problems will arise for classroom teachers unless they have a clear understanding of language and literacy. Although coming to different conclusions about a single model of evaluation, both Dwyer and Lowe & Bintz also argue strongly for such understanding. Without it there is no basis for teachers' judgements except the profiles themselves, which then become the determinants of the curriculum rather than frameworks for viewing learning. This is even more likely to happen if we move to national standards.

Mincham provides insights into how some profiles have been developed in her account of the evolution of procedures for assessing ESL learners in South Australia. She refers particularly to the need to develop some common assessment standards, which highlights a corresponding need for professional development and support for teachers. The UK experiences described by Barrs have some important things to say about the implementation of profiling and its potential for curriculum change which we would do well to heed in Australia. Among them, again, is the need for teacher support and professional development. This is something teachers must collectively insist upon if they encounter political pressure to implement profiling in a hurry.

Given that profiling in some form or other has been established in most states, the question arises as to how teachers can collect and use information in ways that both assist classroom learning and enable them to report first to the major stakeholders, the students and their parents or caregivers, and then to the system. Hayward describes the 'tools' or understandings a teacher must have in order to implement system-wide assessment. She focuses on the assessment of writing as part of the profiling of literacy development in the Northern Territory.

Both Bouffler and Hancock focus on specific classroom behaviours to show how information gathered from day-to-day activities can form the basis of the evaluation necessary for the development of a student's profile. Bouffler looks at the Victorian *Literacy Profiles* and highlights the importance of a theoretical framework for their use. She argues that no externally imposed system of assessment is enough to meet the needs of the classroom teacher. Hancock demonstrates how the teacher can become a researcher. By focusing on one particular aspect of her reading program (Sustained Silent Reading), she was able to develop a system for gathering information about aspects of the reading behaviour of her students and to monitor their development. She was also able to involve them in the process.

There is good reason to involve not only students but their parents or caregivers in the assessment process. If children are to be in control of their own learning, they need to develop the capacity to assess themselves. And if teachers are to retain control of what goes on in their classrooms, they need to be more open and articulate about their classroom practices, particularly with parents. Parents who understand what is going on in their child's classroom are likely to be more supportive of the teacher, both in their acceptance of classroom practice and in public debate. The advantage of parental support becomes evident in the chapter by Fryar, Johnston & Leaker, which describes how they are able to bring all their assessment together in a way that involves teacher, students and parents. I believe that teachers will find this chapter particularly helpful in assisting with the classroom implementation of assessment.

It seems to me that there are many examples of good, well-grounded assessment practices to be found across Australia. The problem is how to identify them and bring them to public attention. It has long been a concern of mine that teachers are not sufficiently articulate and 'up front' about what they are doing. They lack the confidence and assertiveness to take on their detractors. Fehring suggests a way to start to tackle this issue by using the potential of present technology to share good practice among teachers and bring it to the notice of the public.

In the present volatile political and economic climate it is hard to predict what new demands will be made of schools and teachers in the rest of this decade. It is certain, however, that assessment will remain a dominant issue, not only in literacy but in education generally. For teachers of literacy it is also likely to give a new focus to many of the issues of the '70s and '80s.

1 EVALUATION: A POLITICAL ISSUE

Wendy Crebbin

In June 1988 a statement in the *Victorian Parent* predicted that monitoring school and student achievement would become increasingly important over the next few years. It proved to be prophetic. Since then there has been a proliferation of assessment and evaluation documents (such as language and maths profiles in nearly every state), and continuing movement towards a national curriculum and national evaluation.

In 1988 both leading political parties in Victoria had policies aimed at introducing standardised testing to sample the reading, writing and numeracy of students at various grades. This was mirrored in the other states, particularly NSW, where Dr Metherell, then minister for education, announced that he would introduce literacy and numeracy testing for Years 3, 6 and 10. At the same time Mr Carlton, then federal opposition spokesman on education, was arguing for the introduction of standardised testing. He asserted that the lack of a satisfactory performance measurement, combined with lack of competition between students, brought about a loss of incentive and a deterioration in performance, engendering personal insecurity in students and confusion amongst parents and the general public.

The moves to introduce standardised testing were supported by related arguments that there had been a rapid deterioration of educational standards in the '70s and '80s — to the point where Sheridan (1988a) could claim that *the result is one of the worst educational systems in the developed world and one with the least serious monitoring of its own standards.* This view was echoed by opposition politicians and in newspapers throughout the country, where repeated calls for external objective measures of educational achievement were being reported. Along with the call for progressive testing went a demand for the development of minimum standards to be achieved by students before leaving school.

Sheridan's sustained attack on education in the *Australian* (26 March and 9 July 1988) made claims that many readers were unfortunately only too willing to accept. He claimed that teachers were not working hard enough, that students were lazy and knew less than they did in the '70s, that the prevailing approach to education was anti-intellectual and anti-achievement, and that the way to address these problems was through competitive assessment. Although there was much to challenge in his argument and assertions, people accepted them because of their 'commonsense' ring. The type of commonsense which White (1981, p. 48) describes as an *uncritical and largely unconscious way of perceiving and understanding the world* often colours the way we view education, lending writers like Sheridan an authority in the eyes of the public which they do not deserve.

Although more recently the issue of standardised testing has been taken off the agenda for public debate, pushes towards it still continue behind the scenes. However, the changes have provoked some reaction from education groups, such as the Australian Curriculum Studies Association (McTaggart 1991), because the 'commonsense' views argued for by politicians are not the only way of thinking about educational assessment and evaluation. There is, in fact, a range of different views, based on different assumptions and different ideologies about the purposes of education, the contribution of teachers, and what kinds of knowledge students should be learning. Two such views are particularly worth considering here: the traditional or consumption view, and the constructivist approach. Each is political because each is part of a complex set of assumptions about society and human relationships.

Both approaches think of knowledge as a source of power, and both would argue that their way of organising school learning promotes social justice and equity through the development of knowledge. But their interpretation of the nature and sources of that knowledge and equity are very different.

The consumption view of knowledge, favoured by those who promote external objective measurement of learning, basic skill levels and standards, sees knowledge as a product to be consumed. It is based on assumptions that there is a 'body of knowledge' which all students must learn, which is value-free, objective and independent of time or place, and which can be served up by the teacher in discrete units. Such knowledge is usually fragmented, separate from the 'real-life' experiences of students and controlled by others. None the less I suspect that many of us learned to accept a schooling environment with a one-way communication of knowledge, where the teacher was the expert in the classroom, and where neither teachers nor students had much control over the content to be learned because it was usually bound up in pre-established yearly programs, timetables and textbooks.

In the consumption view of schooling, justice and equity are available to all who are willing to compete for the rewards due to high achievers. The onus for achievement is on the individual, and learning and teaching achievement is evaluated in terms of people's capacity to comply with and strive for predetermined goals — goals which are external to the learner, and frequently to the teacher as well. We are all familiar with the kinds of quantitative measurement within relatively fixed categories which go under the names of tests or exams. They have been traditionally applied to this kind of learning to see how much knowledge individuals have consumed. The behaviour required of the learner (and the teacher) is passive consumption, conformity to external pressures and controls, and competition between people of unequal capacities. Furthermore, through the social relations which obtain in consumption-guided classrooms, teachers and learners are inculcated with a particular world view, as theorists such as Giroux (1982), Apple (1982) and Freire (1985) have suggested.

The particular world view that accepts knowledge as a product which can be competed for and evaluated according to pre-determined criteria also accepts that learning can be subjected to managerial values, such as accountability and efficiency. Accordingly, in this view, it is possible to make comparisons between and across different settings, schools and children, without considering any social differences which may exist between them.

By contrast, supporters of the constructivist view of knowledge contend that much of what has traditionally been taught in schools has no intrinsic value, and that there is no sustainable argument to justify giving that particular knowledge a privileged position in our society today. They also suggest that it is difficult to justify the existing discrete divisions between 'subject areas' as well as the claims about a 'body of knowledge'. One of their criticisms of the consumption approach to testing is that students are not only assessed and evaluated in terms of their capacity to reproduce knowledge, but are frequently labelled according to their assumed capacity, so that in time the labels come to define the person. Thus, in a process of blaming the victim, students' failures are always attributed to deficiencies in them, rather than to any defect in the system.

The constructivist view has not only a very different idea about knowledge, but a different political agenda for schooling too. Its proponents argue that education should aim to improve everyone's life chances by promoting fairness and equal consideration for all groups in the community, rather than training people to accept control, conformity and competition (Bates 1983; Freire 1977). Throughout Australia, wherever integrated curriculum, whole language or process writing approaches are used as they were originally conceived, people will be familiar with the kinds of learning approaches used in constructivist education, even if they are not familiar with the label.

In the constructivists' view, all knowledge is understood to be value-laden because it has evolved within particular social, historical and political contexts. They also believe that people come to understand their world by experiencing it and actively thinking about it. Learning, they maintain, is a social activity related to concrete experiences in which shared meanings are developed. The differing cultures, social differences and differences in learning patterns which each person involved brings to the experience are all accepted as part of the shared reality. Within this, the constructivist recognises that ability is not one-dimensional either, but is linked to personal and social factors, such as race, sex, individual characteristics and social background, and can be demonstrated in many ways (Apple 1982; Ladson-Billings 1991). The roles of teachers and learners are therefore active; they all share in the learning, and in setting broad goals which all students will attain. The classroom is a place where students learn to express their own attitudes, feelings and interests, and where the knowledge learned is seen to be relevant to their needs and interests. Constructivist teachers are not concerned about having their students achieve a uniform end product, or having all children of a particular age performing the same task. They are working in complex, diverse and subtle ways to enhance each student's uniqueness. To evaluate such learnings requires a whole range of multidimensional measures, along with individual monitoring of students' learning experiences and their ongoing development of cognitive, creative and social competencies.

As I have suggested previously, the language of both the consumption and constructivist views of knowledge and learning have currency within our schools today, and some of the literacy profiles being used are open to interpretation from either. I have seen the Victorian profiles, for example, being used by a constructivist teacher to encourage the kind of learning she wished to develop with her students, and a teacher with a consumption approach using the same profiles to evaluate her students. In the first case, the student and teacher looked at the student's profile as a means of setting future learning goals, whilst, in the second, the teacher alone made decisions about the students' levels of attainment. It is likely that the profiles in other states are open to similarly differing interpretations.

I believe that teachers need to become aware of the ideological differences between the different teaching approaches because the differences are not a matter of degree — small changes or bigger changes — they are, as I have argued, differences in understandings about knowledge, teachers and learners and the power relationships between them. At the moment few teachers question the conflict between the two very different views of teaching and learning I have outlined. Perhaps it is because, for many teachers, their lived reality takes place within the tension of a dual role — of being both a classroom facilitator and a public evaluator of learning. They are daily trying to balance the needs of their students and the pressures and 'needs' of the education system in which they work. It is also possible that teachers do not recognise the ideological conflict underlying their teaching practices because, in my view, there has been very little, if anything, in their training courses to enable them to unpack the political assumptions or the social impact of different teaching approaches. Here I use the term 'political' to mean far more than just government; rather it has to do with the total organisation of our society, its values and its social assumptions. For, as I have argued, teaching approaches have specific value positions and make specific assumptions about the relationships of individuals within a society. Whichever teaching approach is used, it has the potential for lasting impact on students' lives.

Regardless of such reasons, I suggest, as does Fullan (1991), that in the society of the '90s teachers need to become aware of the political position which they are taking in the ways they teach and assess their students. They also need to take a more active part in the political struggle to define their own and their students' roles for the future. If they do not, I fear that there is a great danger that it will be done for them, in arenas outside education and by people who have agendas similar to those expressed in the newspapers of 1988 — that is, to use standardised testing as a device to attempt once again to increase the external controls over both students and teachers.

References

Apple, M. W. 1982, *Education and Power*, Routledge & Kegan Paul, London.

Bates, R. 1983, *Educational Administration and the Management of Knowledge*, Deakin University Press, Geelong.

Carlton, J. 1988, 'The virtues of honest measurement', *Weekend Australian,* 6 August, p. 26.

Freire, P. 1977, *Pedagogy of the Oppressed*, Penguin Books, Harmondsworth.

Fullan, M. 1991, Educational reform and teacher professionalism, Paper presented at the Australian Council of Educational Administration National Conference, Gold Coast, September.

Giroux, H. 1982, 'Power and resistance in the new sociology of education: Beyond theories of social and cultural reproduction', *Curriculum Perspectives*, vol. 3, no. 2, pp. 197-202.

Ladson-Billings, G. 1990, 'Like lightning in a bottle: Attempting to capture the pedagogical excellence of successful teachers of black students', *Qualitative Studies in Education*, vol. 3, no. 4, pp. 335-44.

McTaggart, R. 1991, 'Towards a new politics of Australian curriculum reform', *Curriculum Perspectives*, vol. 11, no. 3, pp. 14-19.

Sheridan, G. 1988a, 'Why our system is one of the worst in the world', *Weekend Australian,* 26 March, pp. 29-30.

—— 1988b, 'Education reform : Now or never', *Weekend Australian,* 9 July, p. 27.

Victorian Parent 1988, 'Keeping an eye on schools: Monitoring, testing and guidelines', vol. 14, no. 2, p. 8.

White, R. D. 1981, 'Education in bourgeois society: A matter of commonsense', *Interchange,* vol. 11, no. 1, pp. 47-60.

2 UNDERSTANDING EVALUATION

Kaye Lowe & Bill Bintz

While it is necessary to be cautious in assuming parallels between Australian and American education systems, we believe that insights provided by American experience can be useful in helping to understand developing trends in evaluation in Australia. A recent national conference on assessment held at Indiana University provided some important insights into the current state of evaluation in the United States. At this conference it became clear that there is an increasing number of stakeholders struggling to have a voice — indeed, vying for control over evaluation and how it is realised in schools. This growing number of stakeholders includes students, teachers, parents, administrators, policy makers, politicians, test makers, employers, and even real estate agents.

Defining evaluation

Just what is evaluated and how the evaluation is carried out depends on the projected audience. We became more aware as the conference progressed, and emotions ran high, that not only was each group vying for control, but each had a different agenda. These diverse and conflicting agendas are reflected in the following sample of questions taken from conference transcripts.

From a reading/language theorist:
How can you have reliability in assessment if it isn't the same every day?
This question presupposes the need for assessment to be scientifically based, with the emphasis on producing consistent and reliable results.

From a test developer:
How do you report the outcomes of alternative assessment at a state or national level? This question assumes the need to convert qualitative data into statistical information.

From a policy maker:
How can we get reflective instruction and curriculum or teacher judgement reflected in an efficient and useable form in the monitoring function of assessment? [sic] The question appears to assume that evaluation is a monitoring activity that can be condensed to a numerical value.

From a real estate agent:
How can I identify which schools scored the highest on a literacy test in order to use that information to lure the prospective home buyer? Many parents are also interested in the same question. It is not uncommon for families to consider the quality of schools when deciding where to live.

It could be expected that at a conference in which participants represented many sectors of the community, there would be a multitude of ways of defining and justifying evaluation. However, it was obvious that even among language educators there was little consensus when it came to defining evaluation. To test this, we carried out a simple survey: we asked both faculty and students in the language education program at Indiana University to write a short response completing the statement *Evaluation is ....* The following extracts demonstrate the variety of responses we received.

... looking at how things are going.

... the means by which we value something. Evaluation is an active, interactive, proactive aspect of learning, and in that sense it is synonymous with inquiry.

... letting my students know how well they have measured up to a set of criteria or standards.

... assessing value, whether of an experience or a product, according to criteria which have been determined by interested parties, such as teachers, students, parents and community.

... to investigate the outcome of a decision.

The futile search for *the* evaluation model

This survey, together with our experiences as classroom teachers, convinced us that not even educators can agree on what constitutes evaluation. We have both witnessed and participated in the heated discussions that arise when it is suggested that the school report format be modified or discarded. On such occasions we have found ourselves involved not in a simple argument about updating a format, but in a clash of philosophies. What reporting formats attempt to do is to pull together a plurality of philosophies and make them fit within a singular model of evaluation. The eventual format — that which is viewed as most efficient and effective — is frequently norm-referenced and based on standardised testing.

It is clear that attempts to standardise evaluation, like efforts to develop a single report format, ignore two important considerations.

1 Those involved often represent conflicting understandings of evaluation. These understandings, in turn, often represent different views about the nature of knowledge, literacy, learning, curriculum and teaching. For example, those advocating a 'transmission model of learning' — a model which presupposes that there is a predetermined body of knowledge to be mastered, and that learning best occurs when this knowledge is broken down into discrete units — are guided by a very different set of assumptions about evaluation from those who adhere to a 'holistic perspective'. Harste (1989, p. 247) highlights the major difference:

> *According to whole language advocates, knowledge is created through social interaction; it is not something 'out there to be transmitted' ... teaching is not so much transmission as collaboration.*

2 Devising a singular model of evaluation that will meet the needs of all stakeholders is not only impractical but impossible. After all, no model can answer all the questions asked by all those concerned with evaluation — and yet we continue to look for one. Equally we try to perfect answers without considering the validity of the questions. Everybody naturally assumes that they are asking the 'right' questions, but, as we have argued, what is right depends on the audience and purpose for the evaluation. The search for *the* model of evaluation is perpetuated by those for whom a single model is of most benefit. Government agencies, politicians and publishers require manageable, malleable data, and the statistical results of standardised tests provide instant answers. However, the significance of these results to the classroom teacher and their impact on classroom practice is of secondary importance to such groups.

Research in the USA by Carey (1988) concluded that teachers, generally, were unsure why standardised tests were administered, and not one teacher in the survey of over two hundred was found to use the results of this kind of evaluation for any curricular or instructional purpose. An even more discouraging claim was made by Cohen (1989, p. 16), who contended that:

> *Testing procedures already implemented widely in the USA and the UK have not only failed dismally to have any positive effects on school performance; they have also had disastrously toxic effects by producing a negative set of impacts upon schools and their students.*

A model of evaluation formulated outside the learning situation cannot answer the kinds of questions that 'insiders' (i.e. teachers and students, those closest to the learning) are asking. Teachers and students ask questions that are individual, personalised and relate directly to instruction. At the classroom level a model of evaluation designed to encourage and support teachers in asking their own inquiry questions, and then to develop tools for answering them, is not only vital but urgent. For trends indicate that power to determine what will be evaluated, how the evaluation will be done, how the findings will be interpreted and to whom they will be disseminated, is increasingly being assumed by those 'outside' the classroom. Yet policy makers, politicians and administrators are not held directly accountable for the learning of those being assessed, nor for the results of any evaluation. Teachers and students are, and as the primary stakeholders they are disempowered when 'what and how' decisions about evaluation are removed from their control.

Striving for an ultimate model of evaluation not only limits the potential we have for learning from and about our students — it also binds the curriculum to what is being tested. In the United States there is a strong tendency to teach to the test. The curriculum is bound by test preparation, and tests tend to define what gets taught, how it is taught and what is judged as important. Decisions that carry significant consequences are closely aligned with test results. These decisions may include teachers' salaries, students' promotion and graduation, and college admission. While in Australia the situation varies between states, there is the potential in some states for test results to be used to measure the quality of schools and the competence of teachers, as well as student achievement.

What does all this mean for the classroom teacher? We are convinced that it is becoming increasingly important for teachers to articulate their beliefs about learning, teaching and curriculum so that their model of evaluation both reflects and supports them. However, in formulating and articulating these beliefs, it would be all too easy to adopt a defensive stance; to become preoccupied with winning the evaluation battle. When this happens, we cease gaining insights from those most closely involved in learning — the students. It is only through dialogue with students, as well as with parents and peers, that we can improve and expand upon what we currently know.

In resisting the pressure to conform to a single model of evaluation, we would argue that knowledge is neither finite nor static. Nor does it lend itself to being judged by some abstract standard of 'goodness'. Knowledge is socially constituted and dynamic. What we know is a function of the social, political and historical time in which we live. We should not meekly accede to the demands of external groups who doubt the efficacy of schools and regard evaluation as a means of keeping them accountable. We must concentrate on building a system or systems of evaluation that operate from within the philosophy we espouse.

We have to be active in our commitment to educate and convince parents that children are learners and not test-takers. Parents need to be made aware that they deserve more than just the results of 'test-based' evaluation; that, in fact, what they have to contribute is integral to evaluation. Classroom teachers who are prepared to spend time with parents and get them actively involved in their children's learning gain valuable insights into the child as a learner.

We are reminded of this by Narelle's grandfather. Narelle had recently moved into the area and lived with her grandparents. The class assessment procedures used by her Year 2 teacher indicated that she had made unsatisfactory progress during the first two terms. An interview was arranged with her grandfather, at which the teacher explained that although Narelle appeared to be a bright, perceptive child, her results suggested that she was not working to her potential. Her grandfather was able to shed new light on this evaluation. He explained how Narelle had previously been forced to miss a lot of school: 'She had to stay home and take care of her brother. Her mother's a drug addict and at times would leave the children for days. Narelle's been opening cans of baby food since she was three. Reading and writing haven't really been her priority. Survival has!'

Parents, grandparents and significant others can offer crucial information to enhance the limited types of evaluation conducted in the classroom. Narelle's grandfather added a new dimension — a different, more informed way of seeing Narelle, the learner.

Creating a new direction in evaluation: a shift away from perfecting methods

In America, as in Australia, whole language has been instrumental in developing alternative forms of evaluation (anecdotal records, vignettes, systematic observations, periodic sampling, portfolios). However, we would argue that we have for the most part directed our attention towards developing more complex and sophisticated *methods* of evaluation, instead of interrogating and refining the *methodology* that drives these methods.

It is not methods, per se, that enable teachers to assess student growth. It is their understanding of and reflection on the theoretical assumptions about knowledge, learning, literacy, teaching and curriculum that underlie classroom practice.

Halcolm's Evaluation Parable (Patton 1990) provides a good illustration of the difference between methods and methodology. In short, it is a story about a scholar intrigued by the notion of fruit, with which he was not familiar. Having read widely about fruit, he decided to experience it for himself. Armed with a map and details from a 'fruit expert', he arrived at the entrance to an apple orchard. He immediately entered and began to sample blossoms from a range of trees, but despite their beauty he found them distasteful. Disillusioned, he returned to his village, where he announced that fruit was a much overrated food. *Being unable to recognise the difference between the spring blossom and the summer fruit, the scholar never realised that he had not experienced what he was looking for.* (p. 9)

The parallels are only too obvious. As with the scholar, our methods of assessing are not 'wrong'. The scholar managed to pick what he thought was fruit and sampled a variety of trees. Fundamentally it was not what he was doing that was inadequate — it was what he was not doing that was the problem. He needed a completely different understanding, a more informed stance about what constitutes fruit.

We recall the principal who determined the reading ages of children in Years 1–6 by using a 'one-minute' reading test. The test was administered laboriously to all children, and the results were calculated according to the number of words each child could read correctly from a 'graded' passage in one minute.

Although the passages were changed over a period of four years, the rationale for using such an evaluative tool was never explained. The passages were 'improved' in the same way as the scholar moved from one tree to another in search of the tasty blossom. But the same type of reading behaviour was sampled. There was little or no regard for comprehension, strategies employed, interest or knowledge. No attempt was made to understand the miscues made.

We can no longer afford to view evaluation in this way — as a process of perfecting methods, many of which have emerged from outmoded models of learning. Instead we have to go back to the trees (our students), armed with new insights and prepared to make new connections.

If we are to develop alternative models of evaluation, we must start with a methodology grounded in a system of beliefs. For us, whole language provides a theory of knowledge as well as a theory of language, learning and schooling, and so our evaluation must reflect this system of beliefs — our theoretical stance. It is not our intention to expound the philosophies and theories underpinning whole language. Others have done this more adequately than we could here. In what follows we attempt simply to identify the beliefs and assumptions which drive our current methodology. It is our hope that this will serve as a starting point for other teachers to begin articulating and interrogating their own models of evaluation.

Evaluation should be based on an 'insider's' perspective and should be conducted by those closest to the learning process

The ultimate form of evaluation is self-evaluation. We constantly operate within an evaluative framework. We assess the weather and dress accordingly. We assess the conversations we have over lunch and make decisions based on information we have picked up. We evaluate what we eat, and so on. In order to do so, we have developed a set of criteria consistent with our experiences and our expectations of what we want to achieve.

In self-evaluation, we use criteria which are relevant to the circumstances. We trust our judgements and suffer or rejoice in the consequences of our actions. In the real experiences of life, we do not operate within a system that demands results tailored to a set of contrived and mechanistic criteria. For example, if when learning to parachute you fail to leap far enough from the plane and so get caught up in the tail wind, you do not need an expert to tell you that you could improve (though you may need one to show you how!). You evaluate your effort in the light of your experience and will probably decide to take responsibility for finding out what you need to know. But of course the criteria we choose to make judgements about our own success and failure are deeply coloured by the beliefs we have about ourselves as learners.

Students have the capacity for self-evaluation. They begin school after five years of making decisions about what and how they learn. However, this is not to say that as classroom teachers we should not participate in the process. If self-evaluation is to be a viable alternative to testing, then it is important that we work on a collaborative basis alongside our students. Our roles are those of listener, supporter of learning and resource-provider. Students must be given opportunities to be heard and know that what they have to contribute will be valued and respected. When they are given these opportunities, they are able to reflect on what they know and identify what they need to know. Together students and teachers can become informed decision makers about future instruction. Students who are active participants in their own evaluation are more likely to assume responsibility for promoting their own literacy development.

No one learns to be literate unless they become personally involved in literacy. Evaluation as well as instruction must support the fundamental process of involvement — involvement of those most affected by the outcomes. This means that the curriculum should not be fixed, but open to negotiation between student and teacher. Within a negotiated curriculum there is scope for individual students to pose their own inquiry questions and seek to make new and personal connections. But unless evaluation is central to this process and informs instruction, it is likely that a negotiated curriculum will be seen simply as a 'soft' teaching option.

The basis of evaluation is conversation

Without conversation, evaluation of any sort is of little significance. We are reminded of Shona, a six-year-old who produced a piece of writing for her assessment folder. The sample consisted of 'MMWTS'. Shona had taken a reasonable amount of time to produce this specimen, which was below her teacher's expectation. After two years of schooling she appeared not to understand that writing is more than a string of letters. Through conversation, however, she demonstrated another level of understanding and knowledge about the reading-writing process. Pointing to each individual letter, she proudly read 'My Mum went to Sydney'. Fortunately her teacher was perceptive and interested enough to delve beyond the 'product'. But without conversation her teacher would have missed important insights into what Shona knew and understood.

How often when we evaluate do we fail to give our students the opportunity to explain and discuss the logic behind what they have done? *When in doubt, observe and ask questions. When certain, observe at length and ask many more questions.* (Halcolm's Evaluation Laws) Dialogue allows both teacher and student to learn together, rather than grab at the blossom instead of the fruit as the scholar did. But in order to enter into fruitful dialogue, we have to discard the notion that evaluation is about judging or proving something to someone. *There is no burden of proof. There is only the world to experience and understand.* (Patton 1990, p. 7)

Evaluation is a collaborative process

Evaluation is not an isolated entity; it is integral to instruction. When conducted separately from instruction, it is little more than a collecting process. But when students and teachers reflect together on data collected, evaluation becomes more than just a verification of work done — it becomes an ongoing opportunity for inquiry and enhanced understanding.

When teachers and students take the time to plan and work together, learning becomes meaningful. It is negotiated by those involved, not dictated by an authority which not only knows the questions but how they should be answered. By contrast, when evaluation is something that is carried out at the end of a unit of work, the emphasis is simply on recalling facts and information. This sort of evaluation is more closely aligned to the transmission model of learning.

Evaluation is synonymous with learning

Most with a stake in evaluation believe that learning and evaluation are sequential. Learning is planned in advance and then evaluation follows. Ours is a contrary view. We believe that evaluation and learning occur simultaneously: as learners we are engaged in a constant process of learning and evaluation. We do not need to be taught to learn. We evaluate in order to learn and learn in order to evaluate. The relationship between the two is not chronological but dialectical, whereby learning informs evaluation and vice versa. When this relationship exists, evaluation does not perform a monitoring function but acts as a spur to inquiry.

Conclusion

Because it serves many purposes for many people, evaluation is bound to be an emotive issue, and debates about how it should be conducted will continue. In deciding how best to deal with it, teachers must recognise that evaluation implies a philosophical perspective which encompasses learning, literacy and curriculum. Perhaps we should heed John Dewey's advice (1938, p. 5):

> *the business of the philosophy of education does not mean that [it] should attempt to bring about a compromise between opposed schools of thought, to find a via media, nor yet make an eclectic combination of points picked*

out hither and yon from all schools. It means the necessity of the intro-duction of a new order of conceptions leading to new modes of practice.

It is a timely comment. We need to inquire into what constitutes evaluation by discarding our old set of beliefs in favour of new insights. Our starting point should be collaboration with those for whom evaluation has the greatest impact — our students.

References

Carey, R. 1988, Evaluation and whole language, Paper presented to the New York State Education Department Whole Language Conference, Rochester, New York.

Cohen, J. 1989, 'Tests fail to pass their exams', in *Mass Testing: Tonic or Toxin,* ed. G. Shrubb, Education Network, Sydney.

Dewey, J. 1938, *Experience and Education,* Collier Books, New York.

Harste, J. 1989, 'The future of whole language', *Elementary School Journal,* vol. 90, no. 2, pp. 243-49.

Patton, M. Q. 1990, *Qualitative Evaluation and Research Methods,* Sage Public-ations, London.

3 A DIFFICULT BALANCE: WHOLE LANGUAGE IN A TRADITIONAL US SCHOOL

Penny Freppon

As the only first-grade whole language teacher in a US mid-western, urban school, Ellen found that evaluation was the crucial issue when it came to convincing the school principal and district superintendent to allow her to practice whole language teaching. Ellen chose to request permission before implementing her program, and it was then she discovered that the major questions were how she would manage evaluation and how whole language would affect test scores. The children in Ellen's school were from low-income homes, and the school district had an historically strong reliance on standardised testing and skills-based curriculum. Parents, administrators and most fellow teachers in this urban, working-class setting viewed statistics from traditional test measures as documentation of successful literacy learning. Like many professional and lay people, they saw teaching as a predictable, stable task of imparting knowledge and testing learning.

This chapter focuses on Ellen's ways of coping with a traditional system of evaluation which is in conflict with the way she actually thinks and acts in her classroom. It provides an overview of how she manages her teaching within the constraints of the district evaluation program, and describes her behaviour as she evaluates her first graders' language learning. The study is grounded in a transactional theory of language learning (Rosenblatt 1978).

Research in whole language classrooms (Goodman, Goodman & Hood 1989; Harp 1991) suggests that evaluation is best understood by studying the teacher's interactions with children learning to read and write. Hence Ellen's actual thoughts and actions are of interest in this study. Results indicate that she manages evaluation through a complex interplay of observing and reflecting on children's literacy learning and her own teaching.

For the study, children were followed through five months of first grade. Ellen was identified as a whole language teacher through a variety of techniques, including the Theoretical Orientations to Reading Profile, or TORP (DeFord 1979), structured interviews and classroom observations (Freppon 1991). Throughout the autumn I informally interviewed Ellen each week, and twice a week I observed her interactions with the children in her classroom. Audio and video tapes, artefacts and elaborated field notes provided records of these interactions, with a focus on how Ellen managed her whole language program and on some of the evaluation techniques she used to balance her work.

The shape of the problem

School district evaluation policy required Ellen to keep percentage grades in various subjects in her grade book, and to produce quarterly report cards with letter grades. This meant that she had to integrate the specific demands of the school system with what she found to be theoretically and personally accept-able as a whole language teacher.

As I have already indicated, the major issue in Ellen's gaining permission to implement a whole language program was 'covering evaluation' and ensuring that standardised scores would not suffer. Ellen herself explained the situation thus:

> *'My district is very conservative. I consider it curriculum-centred rather than child-centred. Everything [teachers are required to do] is tuned to test results ... standardised evaluation measures are everything. In my first year of my pilot program and in the next year all the principal said to me was, "I thought your kids would test gifted in reading." That comment told me that she saw my program as a catch-all to raise test scores.'*

Throughout her interviews, and in comments she made during classroom observations, Ellen expressed the conflict she felt between the demands of traditional evaluation measures and what she thought was useful to her as a teacher. For example, she noted that children's work samples, kept in port-folios, helped her to monitor progress and shape her teaching to accord with learners' responses. However, the demand to translate actual reading and writing behaviours into numerical values was a continuing problem. As a result Ellen devised a combination of techniques to meet the demands for quantitative data on the children's progress.

Balancing district evaluation demands and whole language teaching

Ellen began the school year with parent questionnaires that provided inform-ation about the children's background in reading. At the same time she inter-viewed all the children about their reading, recording their responses on a separate questionnaire form. (These interviews were repeated at the end of the year.) Samples of both forms are shown opposite.

PARENT'S QUESTIONNAIRE

1. Do you take your child to the library?   ____yes   ✓ no

2. How many times a week or month does your child visit the public
   library?   ____week   ____month

3. When you and your child visit the library, what types of media
   does he/she take out?

   _____books   ____records

   _____films   ____tapes

   _____magazines   ____other (explain)

4. Does your child own a library card?   ____yes   ✓ no

5. Do you own a library card?   ____yes   ✓ no

6. Does your child bring the books home from the library and "read"
   them immediately?   ____yes   ____no

7. Can your child read these books by himself/herself?   ____yes
   ____no

8. How much time do you spend reading a book, magazine, cereal box,
   etc. to your child a day?

   ____15 minutes

   ✓ 1/2 hour

   ____1 hour

   ____1 1/2 hour

   ____more than 1 1/2 hour

9. Does your child read different things to you   ✓ yes   ____no

10. Do you and your child discuss what has been read that day?
    ✓ yes   ____no

READING QUESTIONNAIRE

NAME ████████████████

DATE 8. 31. 90

1. Do you like to read? __No__   Why? I like to look at
   it, but I don't like to read it.

2. What kinds of books do you like to read or listen to?_____

    Goldilocks

3. What do you do when you're reading and you come to something you don't know? I just read it my way. I don't need to know what it says

4. Do you think reading is important? No   Why? _____

    Because I just don't think it's impt.

5. Do you go to another library besides the school library?_____

    Which one?_____ How often?_____ With

    whom? Sister   Do you have a card with

    your name on it? No

6. Is reading hard or easy for you? Easy   Why?_____

    Cause some people teaches me how to read

7. What's your favorite subject in school? dogs, cat   Why?__

    I like...

8. What do you like to do in your spare time? _____

    Read books, bike ride

9. Are you a good reader? Not that much Why? _____

    I just don't know how to read

10. Are you a good writer? Not that much Why? _____

    Cause I don't know how to write the word. I write it my way. Sometimes the sound.

11. What languages do you (or your parents) speak at home?_____

    _____

12. Is your family a reading family? They read the newspaper

13. Is there time and a place for you to read at home? _____

    In my room

Other comments: Sometimes after school.

These documents, along with Ellen's classroom observations, provided personal and affective information about the children's experiences with and responses to written language.

Ellen also carried out mid-year and end-of-year running record analysis of children's oral reading behaviours (Clay 1979) and made notes on the strategies children used, noting particularly those indicating that the child was reading for meaning. Additional running record analysis was done with children who had problems in learning to read.

Ellen integrated some traditional quantitative assessments by using periodic checks from standardised measures provided by basal reader publishers. For example, she had children read from primer and pre-primer books and used evaluation charts provided by the publishers. The numerical values she was required to produce were derived from a combination of running record scores, occasional commercial measures, and her own professional assessment of the child's literacy behaviours.

A great deal of evaluation information was gathered informally and recorded in a large loose-leaf notebook. Daily and weekly notes described children's literacy behaviours: for example, one described how a child was using beginning and ending consonants in his invented spelling, had told his classmates he could read his writing during journal time, and that he sat in the library with a friend looking at a nursery rhyme book and singing the rhymes.

As the school year progressed, Ellen kept careful records of the children's writing and their growing knowledge of letter-sound relationships. The total number of letter-sound relationships used in writing was calculated quarterly. This information, combined with anecdotal notes and samples of children's writing, was used to produce a writing score.

The anecdotal notes and writing samples provided evidence of children's growing ability to produce connected text, and of their effort in writing. Ellen commented in her interviews that monitoring children's writing growth was aided by noting the increase in conventional letter-sound relationships in their stories. She could also predict an increase in reading proficiency by a growing use of letter-sound relationships in writing. Her observations are consistent with Clay's (1979) developmental theory of learning, which holds that conventional reading occurs when children are also beginning to use the alphabetic principle in their writing.

Assigning writing grades proved a continual dilemma for Ellen. Although she never gave very low or failing scores, she did give grades on children's writing after the first half of the year. To handle this aspect of her work, she talked to the children about good writing and showed them examples of stories children had written. She read these stories aloud and explained why she thought they were good.

In brief, Ellen's methods of evaluation combined many whole language techniques with some traditional measures. As a necessary compromise, she produced the kind of evaluation her district demanded while managing her needs as a whole language teacher. Her situation would be intolerable for some teachers — within it she achieved an uneasy peace. Managing a dual system of evaluation requires an innovative and dedicated professional; it is labour-intensive and presents a continual conflict of values. Unfortunately Ellen's story reflects a familiar theme, for many teachers find themselves in similar situations.

Conclusions

Even under the best of circumstances formal evaluation is the bane of most teachers' work. One reason for this is that the nature of pedagogy is inconsistent and complex. It calls on the teacher to be simultaneously mentor and judge, and so how the teacher thinks and acts in the classroom does not follow expected norms (Peterson, Marx & Clark 1978). Recent research (Yinger 1986) indicates that rather than acting as overseers of students, curriculum or quantitative measurement of learning, teachers adapt their actions as they support and assess learners in a recursive and interactive manner. Certainly, exploration of Ellen's thinking and action indicates that she sees evaluation as an inseparable part of learning and the dynamics of her particular classroom. For her, it includes consideration of the children's psychological, academic and social experience. It is *not* a separate step that follows instruction.

Although this discussion provides insights into one teacher's work, I would argue that Ellen's experience is common. Educators like her understand whole language and are willing and able to make it work in schools that require traditional evaluation. Each finds a way of coping. One way Ellen copes is by understanding that her evaluation procedures would be different if she were in a different situation. Her interviews and comments reveal that she knows her evaluation is shaped by the context and culture of her school. Having worked with 'at risk' urban children her entire career, she makes the compromises necessary to continue teaching these children. But at the heart of her evaluation she constructs meaning for herself and her students in ways that are child-centred and consistent with her theoretical understanding. Like all good teachers she does the best she can; she makes her classroom a learning place for the children and herself.

References

Clay, M. M. 1979, *The Early Detection of Reading Difficulties,* Heinemann, Portsmouth, NH.

DeFord, D. E. 1979, A validation study of an instrument to determine a teacher's theoretical orientation to reading instruction, PhD dissertation, University of Indiana, Bloomington.

Freppon, P. A. 1991, 'Children's concepts of the nature and purpose of reading in different instructional settings', *Journal of Reading Behaviour,* vol. 23, pp. 139-63.

Goodman, K. S., Goodman Y. M. & Hood, W. J. 1989, *The Whole Language Evaluation Book,* Heinemann, Portsmouth, NH.

Harp, B. 1991, *Assessment and Evaluation in Whole Language Programs,* Christopher-Gordon, Norwood, NJ.

Peterson, P. L., Marx, R. W. & Clark, C. M. 1978, 'Teacher planning, teacher behaviour, and student achievement', *American Educational Research Journal,* vol. 15, pp. 417-32.

Rosenblatt, L. 1978, *The Reader, the Text, and the Poem,* Southern Illinois University Press, Carbondale, IL.

Yinger, R. J. 1986, 'Examining thought in action: A theoretical and methodological critique of research on interactive teaching', *Teaching and Teacher Education,* vol. 2, pp. 263-82.

4 SYSTEM-WIDE ASSESSMENT: PROFILING PERFORMANCE

John Dwyer

Literacy Standards Falling! Reading Deteriorates! Writing Skills Declining! Spelling — A Disaster Area! Students Lack Communication Skills!

With monotonous regularity, headlines trumpet forth their baleful messages — usually based on limited, often anecdotal data ('An employers' spokesman claimed ...'), or on a limited interpretation of more substantial data.

As teachers, we know that the headlines are not accurate or, at best, tell only part of the story. However, we are frustrated when we try to rebut them because generally we can rely only on our own anecdotal data, which is largely based on the performances of students in our classes. We know that some individuals are having difficulties, but we also know that most cope well with the literacy demands placed on them.

The reduction of this frustration is one answer to the question, 'Why assess at the system level?'

Sound state-wide assessment practices yield reliable data to rebut false claims, or to provide the full story when claims contain some element of truth. At the same time, assessment at the system level can show up strengths or areas that need attention across the system. In addition, it can support teachers not only through its outcomes but through its processes. However, it can only do these things if the policies, practices and procedures involved are filtered through three interlocking sets of guiding principles. The first of these filters is concerned with system-wide issues. The second relates to assessment generally, while the third, vitally important for our purposes, focuses on principles specific to the assessment of language performance.

1 Principles guiding a system-wide assessment program

Acknowledging that the assessment of learning is always linked with social, economic and political agendas outside the immediate educational context, a system-wide assessment program should inform significant stakeholders about what is being achieved, as well as defining areas at risk and helping to plan remedies. It should be collaborative rather than hierarchical: that is, schools, teachers and administrators should support and inform each other, with schools and teachers involved in the collection and analysis of data. A sound, system-wide assessment program will be a resource for classroom teachers, defining performance standards and informing classroom assessment practices. It will develop the capacity of teachers to become active, effective assessors of their students and themselves.

Such a program must be open for the consideration and scrutiny of all stakeholders. So it must, for example, make explicit the amount, nature, requirements and timing of assessment practices. It should provide both qualitative and quantitative data in ways which avoid distorting good teaching practice. Finally, it must be cost-effective in terms of money and time.

2 Principles which underpin assessment in general

Effective assessment is an integral, purposeful part of the educational process, continually providing both 'feedback' and 'feedforward'. It enables students to demonstrate what they know and guides their future learning. However, to do this, its practices must be in harmony with the characteristics, abilities and interests of the groups of students being assessed. Its instruments, processes and reported outcomes need to be fair to all, including girls and students from differing social and cultural backgrounds.

Effective assessment practices provide opportunities for self-assessment and evaluation and encourage teachers and students to see themselves as active participants. A sound assessment program pays attention to process as well as product and incorporates, as far as practical, a variety of assessment tasks and activities. It ensures that reporting is consistent with the assessment measures used and meaningful to the targeted audiences. The limitations of any assessment methodology will be admitted, and equally there will be an acknowledgement that policies and practices are critically dependent on the quality of interpretation of the results obtained.

3 Principles guiding the assessment of language performance

Practices for assessing language performance can and should always be traced back to an underlying model of language. This model should be as open for inspection as the results obtained through the assessment program. Most of us would agree that a sound model would make the following assumptions about the nature of language: using language is a purposeful, social activity and implies an audience; the four modes of language are closely interrelated; language form is determined by its function.

Language is shaped according to the context of its use. Thus authentic assessment of language performance demands a search for authentic contexts and cross-curricular emphases. It also requires procedures which allow both holistic and analytical approaches to what is being assessed.

Profiling: a response to the principles

These sets of principles, or filters, are daunting. It is certain that 'tick-the-box' and 'fill-the-gap' types of assessment exercise will not pass. However, one promising approach, currently receiving widespread attention in Australia, is subject profiling. Recently the Australian Co-operative Assessment Program (ACAP) management committee commenced a national feasibility study on subject profiling. The project outline makes the following points:

> *A subject profile is an agreed description of student outcomes in relation to elements of a subject such that student progress can be recorded.*
>
> • *It is desirable that Australasian education systems develop a shared language for communicating student achievements; reduce unnecessary differences and the duplication of effort in assessing and reporting outcomes; and benefit from each other's experience and work in this area.*
>
> • *Subject profiles should be derived from and reinforce agreed curriculum priorities and should be consistent with the content and processes of the curriculum in the subject areas for which they are to be developed.*
>
> • *Subject profiles should provide a framework which can be used by teachers in classrooms to chart the progress of individual learners, by schools to report to their communities and provide a framework for systems' reporting on student performance as well as be amenable to reporting student achievement at the national level.*
>
> • *Subject profiles should support students' learning by providing students and their parents with specific information about their progress in a subject throughout the compulsory years of schooling, in relation to clear agreed national descriptions of levels of achievement for particular subject areas. This information will also inform teachers about the efficacy of the learning and teaching program in relation to students' particular needs.*
>
> • *Subject profiles should describe students' levels of achievement ('standards referencing') and where they stand in relation to relevant student populations.*
>
> • *The levels of achievement should relate to the bands of schooling as described in the national curriculum mapping exercise.* (ACAP 1990)

Subject profiling, then, is a means of gathering information, using school-based processes, and of aggregating this information in order to provide a profile of performance of students studying particular subjects at defined levels.

The information gathered should be capable of being used for several purposes. Ideally, it should be *formative*, so that an individual's achievements can be recognised, discussed and used to plan further learning. It should be *diagnostic*, so that an individual's difficulties can be identified, and help and guidance provided. It should be *summative,* so that the overall achievement of the individual can be recorded systematically, and it should be *evaluative,* so that aspects of the educational program of a school, region or education system can be assessed and reported upon.

Current approaches to subject profiling include two other important and related elements: viz. any assessment process and method must reflect the agreed aspects of a subject curriculum, and teacher development should be an important part of the overall process. Thus the national subject profiles project proposes that achievement levels in any subject should be determined by looking at good practice and consulting about it. This is regarded as the best way to proceed because it recognises that the judgement and experience of teachers are critical to the assessment of students' achievement and growth.

Profiling language performance

Against this conceptual background there are currently at least three different language profile approaches in use in Australia: the Tasmanian *Pathways of Language Development* program, the Victorian *Literacy Profiles* program, and programs in New South Wales, Queensland and Western Australia which have used a testing procedure that plots individual item difficulty and individual student achievement on a common measurement scale. (The scale can then be used to describe the language aspects tested and the performance standards achieved.) The first might be characterised as a 'mapping' profile, the second as a 'benchmarks' profile and the third as a 'performance' profile. In various ways all three approaches draw on the judgement and experience of teachers.

A mapping profile

In Tasmania, *Pathways of Language Development* grew out of the need of some teachers to find a framework for their observation and planning which was compatible with a holistic approach to language development. These teachers were aware of the richness of data provided by their own observations of students as language users, and they knew that this information was more valuable than that provided by off-the-shelf standardised tests. So they developed *Pathways* as a way to use the information to guide the ongoing monitoring and assessment of students' language development. They suggested that students progress along 'pathways' as they develop language, and that since each student's language is unique, there is no fixed pathway. Each student gains progressive control of language processes and becomes increasingly independent in using and understanding them.

The *Pathways* framework incorporates five interdependent strands: language purposes, language contexts, language conventions, language and feeling, and language and thought. These strands serve to organise a range of

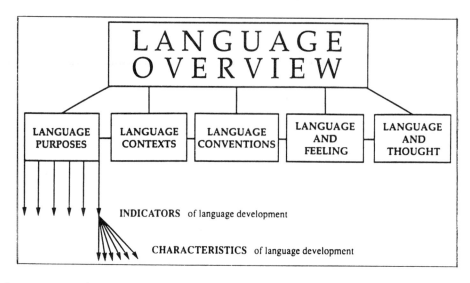

indicators, each representing an aspect of language use identified by the classroom research of a number of teachers. Each strand has its own chart displaying the indicators which belong to it and listing some of their characteristics. Detailed material supporting each indicator includes questions to focus observations when evaluating a student's learning, links with other indicators and suggested teaching strategies (see examples opposite).

There is no 'right' way to use the materials, but a number of suggestions have been provided. For example, teachers are encouraged to make a chart showing indicators of one or other strand and then to negotiate work with students based on a chosen indicator. Alternatively, teachers can refer to appropriate indicators and characteristics in conferences and encourage students to use the indicators in evaluating their own work.

Pathways can be used with parents. For instance, the teacher can prepare a book of examples of a student's writing and annotate each one by referring to the relevant indicators. *Pathways* can also be used as a guide in preparing written reports to parents, or the overview chart can be used when discussing a student's progress with parents.

By mapping a student's progress within each strand, an individual profile can be developed. And while the materials were developed for monitoring and reporting on individual progress, and to provide a framework for planning and implementing effective classroom programs and practices, it would be possible to aggregate individual profiles in such a way that judgements could be made about what had been achieved within each strand across a school, region or system.

This profiling approach is certainly consistent with the sets of principles outlined above. In particular, it is derived from and supports a clearly stated model of language. It is collaborative, drawing heavily on teachers' expertise while involving both teachers and learners as data gatherers and assessors. It

POSES QUESTIONS AND FORMULATES HYPOTHESES

Does the student:
- display an understanding of open and closed questions?
- demonstrate a sensitivity to appropriate timing of questions?
- participate in discussions intended to solve real or imaginary problems?
- consider and compare alternative solutions, plans of action and responses?
- offer divergent solutions to problems?
- ask pertinent questions?
- ask questions to clarify issues?
- try out possible solutions?
- identify problems in literature and offer possible solutions?
- formulate hypotheses by synthesising ideas from various sources?
- articulate the bases of hypotheses?

Links with other indicators
- Adjusts concepts to integrate new learning
- Obtains and organises information to suit purpose
- Reviews impressions, assumptions and understandings
- Organises ideas coherently

Links with pre-independent indicators
- Seeks response by questioning
- Uses cueing systems and strategies in flexible ways to gain meaning from print

---

Suggested strategies
Within a whole language program in which students are encouraged to make explicit for themselves and others what they are thinking and learning:
- demonstrate and discuss the effectiveness of various questioning techniques during shared reading, class discussions, individual and small group conferences
- demonstrate the testing of hypotheses by consulting a variety of resources
- provide opportunities for students to explain the bases of hypotheses
- pose challenges for small groups which require them to formulate possible hypotheses; discuss and explore their appropriateness
- identify a problem faced by a character in a book or film and discuss alternative solutions
- invite each student to write a narrative to the point at which a complication emerges, and ask a partner to find a resolution
- discuss social, economic, political and moral issues and explore possible solutions
- explore and evaluate historical problems and their resolutions

allows for the use of a variety of assessment tasks and activities and provides a framework for meaningful reporting. While, to date, it has been used to develop individual profiles, it would be possible to devise a methodology for aggregating these to produce school or system-wide profiles of language performance, which could be related to age or grade, if necessary, to establish performance standards.

A benchmarks profile

A second profiling approach, a benchmarks approach, is exemplified by the Victorian *Literacy Profiles* project. This is also the approach used with the national curriculum and national assessment in the UK.

In the Victorian model, a literacy profile is an array of information that describes and evaluates a student's reading and writing. It encompasses not only strategies and accomplishments, but also attitudes and interests in the field of literacy. Information recorded for reading can range from 'concepts about print' to 'responses to texts'. Writing information can range from 'spelling strategies' to 'purposes for writing'.

Literacy Profiles allows for a comprehensive picture of growth in literacy. Information may be drawn from interviews with students or parents, from checklists or from tests. However, the richest and most valid source is teacher observation of students who are actually reading and writing. Developed by teachers, the profiles demonstrate that the intuitive assessments and professional judgements made by teachers can accurately define the growth and development of literacy among learners.

The material in the Handbook includes descriptions of literacy learning behaviours noted by teachers in a variety of schools. It also includes descriptions of classroom contexts and activities in which these behaviours are commonly observable. It makes provision for recording observations and offers a guide to assessing and reporting on students' development in literacy.

Literacy Profiles contains bands (or benchmarks) representing reading and writing behaviours which tend to occur at about the same time in a learner's development. A sample band is reproduced opposite. The indicators in the bands are all framed in positive terms, and the bands themselves have breadth and scope, offering much more information than is yielded by standardised tests. However, the published bands are not exhaustive, and teachers are encouraged to extend the profile by adding further indicators of development. While the materials have been developed to produce individual profiles, again it is possible to aggregate these to define system-wide standards of literacy performance.

Like *Pathways, Literacy Profiles* was developed collaboratively. At workshops teachers suggested and defined indicators of literacy, and when they returned to their classrooms, they made observations to validate them. Students' reading and writing behaviours were surveyed to determine the order of

---

WRITING BAND   E   ☐

What the writer does ☐ ————————————————————

Edits work to a point where others can read it; corrects common
   spelling errors, punctuation and grammatical errors.

Develops ideas into paragraphs.

Uses a dictionary, thesaurus, word checker, etc. to extend and check
   vocabulary for writing.

What the writing shows ☐ ————————————————————

Sentences have ideas that flow.

Paragraphs have a cohesive structure.

Ability to present relationships and to argue or persuade.

Message in expository and argumentative writing can be identified by
   others but some information may be omitted.

Brief passages written, with clear meaning, accuracy of spelling and apt
   punctuation.

Appropriate shifts from first to third person in writing.

Consistent use of the correct tense.

Appropriate vocabulary for familiar audiences such as peers, younger
   children or adults with only occasional inappropriate word choice.

Compound sentences—using conjunctions.

Variations of letters, print styles or fonts.

A print style appropriate to task.

Consistent handwriting style.

Use of Writing ☐ ————————————————————

Writes a properly sequenced text which has a convincing setting.

Creates characters from imagination.

---

development of the indicators, which were then clustered into bands. After teachers, consultants and language specialists had met to provide comment, field testing of the revised bands was carried out in schools, resulting in more feedback and revision. Discussions were held with parents and teachers to gather ideas and advice on the use of the bands for assessment and reporting. A project was set up to identify assessment tasks which would strengthen the reliability of the whole procedure.

This last point raises an issue of some difficulty which is inherent in both the *Pathways* and the *Literacy Profiles* approaches: their value as assessment and reporting tools relies heavily on the accuracy and consistency of teachers' interpretations of the indicators and the judgements they make against them.

In the UK, where the national curriculum has been defined in terms of benchmarks called 'attainment targets', a considerable amount of work has gone into the development of Student Assessment Tasks (SATs), to be administered by teachers in their own classrooms to moderate their own ongoing assessment of students' performance. In a report on the first phase of the development of these SATs, the researchers found that some statements of attainment were capable of being *applied* differently even when teachers agreed on what they meant.

It seems that while teachers are accustomed to assessment in some form or other, many of us need advice on ways of recording, on the spot, transient aspects of students' performance, such as speaking, listening and hypothesising. We also need advice on ways of gathering information. Four factors seem to be central here: classroom organisation and management, knowledge of students, understanding of the materials and approaches, and knowing when to intervene.

Teachers capable of managing the classroom in such a way that they can spend longer periods with small groups or individuals are able to make better observations and more carefully considered judgements. Clearly the availability of ancillary support is an important consideration.

Teachers who have established good relationships with their students, and who have a knowledge of their general level of communication skills and their personalities, are better at providing opportunities for them to demonstrate evidence of their attainments. Qualities such as patience, insight and 'real' listening to what students say also help to put assessment on a sounder base.

It is no doubt self-evident that unless we know and understand the procedures to be used, any assessment we undertake will lack focus. It is here that any ambiguities in the statements of attainment become important. There is evidence to suggest that assessments are better and more reliable when such statements are translated into context-specific behaviours. *Pathways* and *Literacy Profiles* materials certainly attempt to do this.

Finally, many teachers seem unaccustomed to taking on an observer or researcher role in their classrooms. Many of us find difficulty in standing back and making observations without feeling the urge to intervene. Some of us lack skills when intervention is necessary, particularly the skills of open-ended questioning. Sometimes we have difficulty in sustaining the consistency of our support and the quality of our intervention, which can lead to inequalities in the opportunities we give students to show what they can do.

What is clear overall is that while it is possible to rely on teachers' experience and contributions in establishing bands of performance, many teachers will require support and training to ensure accuracy and consistency in their interpretations of the indicators, and in the judgements they make against them. (See White 1990 and NFER Consortium 1989.)

A performance profile

The third approach is the performance profile used in New South Wales, Western Australia and Queensland. As I have been closely involved with the Queensland program, I will use it to exemplify this approach.

An early stage in the evolution of the Queensland program was the development of broad general frameworks to map the key concepts and process of reading and writing of the Years 1-10 English Language Arts curriculum. From these general frameworks, monitoring frameworks were developed to identify the specific aspects of reading and writing which would be assessed. The Reading Assessment Grid is an example.

READING ASSESSMENT GRID

Aspects of reading are measured which depend on a range of **THINKING PROCESSES** and **SKILLS** and the application of pupils' **KNOWLEDGE** associated with reading. The measures are obtained using a variety of **Genres** and **Stimulus Materials** within different **Test Approaches.** The actual measures are assessed and reported on an Overall Performance basis and on Factual Comprehension, Inferential Comprehension and Research Skills clusters.

The **PROCESSES, SKILLS** and **KNOWLEDGE** covered relate to the Reading Curriculum Structure.

The **PROCESSES** include: recalling, reflecting, questioning, analysing, synthesising, hypothesising, evaluating, inferring and imagining.

The **SKILLS** covered are:
*   *interpreting language features* such as: generic structure, cohesion, vocabulary, grammar, paragraphing and punctuation; and
*   *using communicative procedures* such as: checking, using contextual cues, skimming and scanning, and summarising and integrating.

The **KNOWLEDGE** relates to knowledge about genre and social context and language features.

Genres used are broadly clustered as:
*   NARRATIVE including short stories and descriptive passages; and
*   NON-NARRATIVE including descriptive paragraphs, maps, indexes and recipes.

Stimulus Materials to be used include: narrative passages, expository articles, descriptive articles, advertisements, poetry, maps, title pages, indexes and newspaper articles.

Test Approaches to be used include: multiple choice, true/false questions, short answer questions, longer written answers, cloze exercises and completion of tables of information.

		NARRATIVE (including short stories and descriptive passages)	NON-NARRATIVE (including descriptive paragraphs, maps, indexes and recipes)
REPORTING LEVELS	Overall Performance		
	Factual Comprehension		
	Inferential Comprehension		
	Research Skills		

Aspects of the Reading Curriculum Structure which are not covered by the Reading Assessment Grid are Attitudes and pupils' Knowledge about their own attitudes, thinking processes, skills and knowledge.

Against these frameworks a collection of tasks and items was developed. Groups of teachers, language consultants, curriculum writers, tertiary educators and ACER consultants and test developers suggested, reviewed and critically discussed the test tasks to ensure they were worthwhile, with strong curriculum relevance and classroom credibility. The groups examined the range and balance of assessment formats and their content. They searched the materials for any possible gender, cultural or location bias, and considered the relevance of tasks both to year level and classroom practice. They checked the level of the reading and writing demands of individual tasks, the familiarity of the content of stimulus materials, and the appropriateness of instructions, art-work and layout. This review phase was followed by field trials and further refinements. The real strength of the development process lay in the extensive expertise and breadth of experience available amongst those involved.

Reading and writing were dealt with together and the assessment tasks were presented in the form of booklets, with each booklet usually containing three tasks (one writing, two reading). Six test booklets were developed at each target year level (Years 5, 7 and 9). While tasks in all booklets at each level were of approximately similar standard, with similar demands, the number of different booklets allowed for a broad range of genres and language features to be assessed.

After the tests had been used state-wide and the results of over 14000 stud-ents had become available, the performance demands of the various tasks and subtasks were established and mapped on an overall performance scale. Care-ful inspection of this scale led to the identification of cut-off points for per-formance levels and the development of a performance profile in which each level was cumulative, with the higher levels subsuming the lower. To illustrate this, the overall reading performance scale across Years 5, 7 and 9 is outlined in the table opposite.

Such a profile has value for teachers. It provides a performance-based set of standards against which we can assess the work produced by students in our own classes. To assist with this, the report on results describes how the mark-ing was carried out and provides examples of students' work by way of illustration. In addition, detailed reviews of most tasks and subtasks (also illustrated with examples of students' work) are included, providing teachers with a task item bank, a methodology for assessment and a marking schema which can be used in their own classrooms.

Conclusion

The three profiling approaches described in this chapter are in harmony with the three sets of principles outlined at the beginning. They have the capacity to meet assessment requirements at the student, class, school or system level. To varying degrees they are collaborative, drawing on teacher expertise and involving teachers in the assessment process. They all have the potential to develop teachers' skills as active, effective assessors, and to provide both quantitative and qualitative data. They all use processes and techniques which reflect and support good teaching practice, and can be seen as an integral, purposeful part of the education process. They enable teachers to demonstrate what students do *know* and can *do*. They allow for a variety of data-gathering activities and techniques and facilitate fair and meaningful reporting of outcomes. They are built on worthwhile models of language and allow for both holistic and analytic assessment. But perhaps their greatest strength is the scope they offer teachers to influence system-wide assessment;

Synopsis of overall reading levels

5

- forming cogently reasoned hypotheses, predictions and conclusions based on explicit and implicit information
- drawing logical inferences from scattered and implicit information
- synthesising and explaining complex and implicit information
- justifying hypotheses about an author's intent or opinion, or a character's thoughts
- demonstrating an appreciation of subtleties

4

- interpreting challenging vocabulary and language use through textual and contextual clues
- explaining and paraphrasing implied and indirect causal relationships
- logically sequencing scattered information and descriptions of events
- explaining an author's opinion and predicting a character's probable thoughts, emotions and actions
- appreciating the application of some authorial techniques and their intended effects

3

- extracting, synthesising and integrating explicit and implicit information
- drawing simple conclusions and forming rudimentary judgments, hypotheses and predictions
- using textual and contextual clues to determine the meaning of vocabulary or idiom
- identifying the main idea and an author's intent or opinion

2

- locating and synthesising explicit information
- recognising paraphrased information
- demonstrating some awareness of the effects of stylistic techniques
- applying reference information
- recognising causal and factual relationships

1

- locating and retrieving explicit information from text and in reference form
- exhibiting awareness of an author's intent and main idea
- recognising overt causal relationships
- interpreting unfamiliar vocabulary using distinct contextual clues
- drawing simple inferences from explicit information

to manage, in their own classrooms, procedures related to system-wide assessment; to negotiate and interpret system-wide results, and to specify their own in-service needs as a consequence.

References

ACAP [Australian Cooperative Assessment Program] 1990, A conceptual framework for the development of subject profiles, Unpublished paper, November.

NFER [National Foundation for Educational Research] Consortium 1989, *The Development of Standard Assessment Tasks for Key Stage 1: Report on First Phase Development,* NFER & Nelson, Slough.

Review and Evaluation Directorate, Queensland Department of Education 1991, *Assessment of Student Performance 1990: Aspects of Reading and Writing: Overall Results,* Brisbane.

Schools Program Division, Victorian Ministry of Education 1990, *Literacy Profiles Handbook: Assessing and Reporting Literacy Development,* The Education Shop, Melbourne.

Tasmanian Department of Education and the Arts 1989, *Pathways of Language Development,* 2nd edn, Hobart.

White, J. 1990, Essential concepts of assessment, Paper presented to 4th National TESOL Conference, Brisbane, 17 August.

5 ASSESSING THE ENGLISH LANGUAGE NEEDS OF ESL STUDENTS

Lexie Mincham

This chapter outlines an approach to language assessment which has the potential to serve a range of different purposes at classroom, school and system level. The ESL Student Needs Assessment Procedures (SNAP), described below, have been developed in South Australia by ESL and mainstream teachers working in partnership with consultants from the Education Department's ESL Curriculum Project. While the procedures have been specifically designed to identify the English language needs of ESL children, teachers have found them useful in analysing the oral and written language abilities of all learners in the primary years of schooling.

The approach taken is particularly interesting in that it provides teachers with clear guidance about how to assess children's work in a range of common classroom learning activities. The information obtained can then be used by teachers to modify their programs to suit children's different learning needs. It also serves as a basis for giving children specific feedback about their progress and about ways in which they can improve their performance. Teachers are able to help children establish clear and understandable goals for learning and develop strategies for monitoring and evaluating their own and others' progress, using simplified versions of the assessment procedures.

The origins of SNAP

In addition, teachers can report their assessment of children's performance on any activity in terms of a 'global' rating, using a scale rising from 1 to 5. Children's performance in a range of activities can then be aggregated, and the resulting information can be used by education authorities to help make decisions about the special support needs of particular groups of learners. In fact, it was chiefly this function of assessment in advising of children's needs at system level that led to the development of SNAP.

A review of the South Australian ESL program in 1987 found that it was failing to meet the needs of many children under the prevailing criteria for allocating specialist staff to schools. The criteria were simple: for ESL children resident in Australia between one and five years, schools could have one full-time specialist teacher per 36 children; for those resident over five years, the ratio declined to one teacher per 200 children.

As many teachers have recognised, length of residence is a crude and inadequate criterion. It takes no account of such crucial factors as children's previous education and language learning experience (both in English and in their first language), their personal well-being, their socio-economic circumstances and the language(s) spoken at home. It denies any cross-cultural issues related to the varying ways that particular cultures use language to perform a range of functions. And it ignores the distinction between informal or 'playground' English, in which children may become fluent quite quickly, and the language demands of the classroom, which are much more complex and abstract, involve writing, and may take upwards of five years to master. (See *Learning to Learn in a Second Language* [Gibbons 1991], especially Chapters 1 and 2.)

A portfolio approach

SNAP, then, was grounded in a determination to find out what the real needs of ESL learners were. From the outset the teachers and project consultants recognised the importance of providing a means of assessment which would not only identify language needs accurately, but could also be used by all primary teachers — not simply those with specialist expertise in ESL. It was also important to ensure that the procedures could be used within the context of normal classroom learning activities, so as to limit the amount of extra work that might be needed in planning and carrying them out.

For these reasons, it was decided to adopt a portfolio approach. This would be compatible with many teachers' existing assessment practices and would allow them both to gather information over a period of time and report on it for resourcing purposes in mid-year if required.

For resourcing purposes, the procedures require an assessment to be made of the language needs of each student for whom English is a second language, not just those who are recently arrived or who stand out as needing support. In some cases children's needs are not identified as being language-related in the first instance, but are thought to be caused by specific learning difficulties or to be the result of poor motivation or behaviour problems. While these may be compounding factors, an assessment of a child's oral and written language can reveal important underlying information, which the teacher can then use to assist the child's development in English. To help teachers identify the full range of ESL children, the procedures contain suggestions for gathering personal information and a form that can be used to record the information for school purposes (such as providing interpreters for parent interview evenings).

What should be included in the portfolio ?

As already indicated, the assessment is made on the basis of children's oral and written performance in a range of typical classroom learning activities. While this is not to deny the importance of gathering information about such things as children's attitudes and learning processes, it serves to emphasise just how much essential information can be gained about children's specific language needs through the detailed analysis of samples of actual language use.

In deciding what should be included in the portfolio, the teachers and project consultants were guided by this statement:

> *In all areas of the school curriculum and in the wider community, learners are engaged in using language to widen their networks of interpersonal relations; to gain access to, process and use information; to think critically; to reflect and to express themselves imaginatively and cretively.*
> (SA Education Dept 1990, p. 7)

Within these dimensions the procedures would need to reflect a range of language use as defined in *Australian Language Levels Guidelines* (Scarino, Vale & McKay 1988). So the teachers set about identifying what they felt were the most common genres across the curriculum, giving priority to what they saw as being particularly relevant at the different year levels. They then turned to drafting criteria to be used in assessing children's performance in each of the activities they had selected, which are listed below.

Portfolio requirements – Reception to Year 2

Oral
2 samples taken from:

retelling a story
activity-sharing
morning talks

Written
2 samples made up of:

a recount *and*
a report

Portfolio requirements – Years 3 and 4

Oral
2 samples taken from:

retelling a story
activity-sharing
news

Written
2 samples made up of:

a report *and*
a narrative *or*
a procedure

Portfolio requirements – Years 5 to 7

Oral

2 samples taken from:

retelling a story
reporting on a process
giving an opinion

Written

3 samples made up of:

a recount *and*
an argument *and*
a narrative *or* a report

(SA Education Dept 1990, p. 73)

In working on the activities to be included for the written assessment, the teachers drew largely on work already being done by the NSW Disadvantaged Schools Program and the Literacy and Education Research Network. *Exploring How Texts Work* (Derewianka 1990) was also an important resource, as was *Let's Talk* (Rowe 1989) for oral language.

Field trials

Once the draft assessment forms had been completed and guidelines decided upon for conducting the procedures, the full range of oral and written activities was trialled extensively in schools. (More than seventy ESL and mainstream teachers were involved in the various stages associated with the development and trialling of the procedures.) During the trialling stage, samples of children's work were gathered and assessed, both by teachers working individually and then as part of a group moderation process. (Unfortunately, despite the loss of phonological features such as rhythm and intonation, the taped oral samples had to be transcribed, since the classroom recordings were not clear enough to be included in the teacher support materials.) As a result of the trialling, refinements were incorporated in the draft criteria and guidelines were drawn up for training teachers to use the materials.

Judging a child's performance

Assessment forms are provided to give teachers specific criteria for judging a child's performance in any of the selected activities. The forms allow assessment to be made at an analytical level (that is, according to the components of the task), as well as at an holistic level (that is, judging the child's overall performance on the task and using a global rating from 1 to 5). Space is provided for recording particular points which might form the basis of future teaching or the focus for special attention, as well as for making general comments which can be used in reporting to parents and caregivers.

The assessment procedures can be used at any stage of the curriculum cycle. For example, they can be used to determine what children can already do, as a starting point in the planning of any teaching-learning activity. (In such cases the assessment should reflect what children are able to do without support.) Equally they can be used to assess children's learning at the end of a unit of work or program of study.

Ensuring a common standard

It was felt that some means of ensuring common assessment standards among teachers was important, particularly if the assessment information was to be used outside the immediate school context. Some teachers have had little or no experience of dealing with second language learners; others have classes which are made up of children from a variety of ethnic backgrounds. Some have taught mainly new-arrivals; others may have mainly taught children who were born in Australia but come from homes where little or no English is spoken, or children whose schooling has been disrupted by overseas travel, etc. Many teachers will have experienced a combination of these possibilities.

  Accordingly, in order to ensure that all teachers have a common view of what is an acceptable standard of performance, moderated samples of children's work are provided for each of the activities (three examples of these are shown in the following six pages). Because children may receive the same rating on an activity but have a slightly different assessment profile, several samples of work have been provided for each rating from 1 to 5. Further, to ensure that the full range of performance is represented in the samples, work from English background speakers has been included. Where possible, a brief profile of each child's language background is given as well.

Professional development and curriculum change

The following comments reflect some of the positive results experienced by teachers participating in the development and trialling of the procedures.

> *Focusing on a pre-determined set of criteria helped in becoming more aware of learners' individual needs.*

> *Without the criteria it was easy to revert to assessing surface features such as spelling, rather than [focusing] on the ways in which students are learning to make meaning.*

> *The focus on genre-based activities was relevant to primary classroom activities and easy to fit in.*

> *I recognised some characteristics of individual children I hadn't quite been able to put my finger on before.*

> *... decided I must do more oral work, particularly in small groups.*

> *I now have higher expectations of what young children are capable of achieving in a range of writing.*

ORAL LANGUAGE ASSESSMENT

A morning talk

The first text is a morning talk given by Khoa. Khoa was born in Australia and is of Vietnamese background. He is six years old and in his first year of school. Khoa's teacher tells us that, as yet, Khoa is very shy when speaking in front of a large group and that the sample provided here was taken in a small group situation. [Notes: The marking ... represents hesitations in the child's speech. The letters K, T and S indicate who is speaking, i.e. Khoa, the teacher and another student.]

K   *Well, when I went fishing ... a ... nd and my Dad did ... my Dad didn't get some fish. And my Mum get ... got six fish ... Um ... My sister saw a rat first and I saw it ... and we trina [tried to] get that rat out first and the hardest rock ... the hardy rock. And any questions?*

T   *Did you get the rat out?*

K   *Killed 'm.*

S   *Khoa, is the crab die?*

Oral Language Assessment Activity - MORNING TALKS   YEARS R-2

Name of Student: *Khoa*   Year Level: *Rec.* Class: Date:

Task: *Giving a morning talk*   Context: *Small group*

Description of activity: Students recount a personal experience or describe an event, object or topic of personal interest.

Criteria (Tick appropriate box)	Very Competent	Competent	Limited Competence	Not Yet	Comments
Ability to carry out the task Did the student:					
• speak appropriately for audience and purpose			✓		*small group only*
• complete the task independently, ie with minimal support		✓			*little prompting*
Structure and Organisation Did the student:					
• set the scene e.g. "On Saturday I..."			✓		
• relate events or describe objects clearly and with sufficient detail			✓		
• generally keep "on topic"		✓			
Language Features Did the student:					
• use appropriate tense; eg "drew" not "drawed", "have drawn" not "have drawed"			✓		*get → got* *went* *didn't get*
• use specific vocabulary; eg "tiger," "shovel"			✓		
• use a range of descriptive words and phrases; eg verbs, adjectives, adverbs			✓		*hardest rock → hardy rock*
• use reference items: eg, pronouns; he, she, it and articles; a, the		✓			
• use a range of connectives; eg, first, then, so, because			✓		*when, and*
Communication Skills Did the student:					
• speak fluently without too many hesitations; eg "um"....."er"			✓		
• speak clearly; eg pronounce words accurately, sound plurals and verb endings		✓			*trina*
• self-correct; eg "... on Friday ... no, on Thursday ..."			✓		*get → got, but didn't get some*
• show an awareness of audience by:					
- selecting an interesting event or object		✓			
- using visuals/support materials					*n/a*
- using appropriate body language		✓			
• answer audience questions effectively (optional)			✓		*limited info.*

General Comments:
- Khoa is confident in small group situations only — was able to speak without prompting from the teacher.
- Needs support in extending his introductory statement to include more detail e.g. time and place of the event.
- Relies mainly on use of 'and' as a connective.
- Approximates some words e.g. 'trina' for 'were trying to'/ 'tried to'.
- Meaning of 'the hardest rock' unclear.
- Responds to question from teacher, but does not offer more detail.
  • Needs modelling provided by other competent English speakers in the class
  • Could be encouraged to record talks on tape and play back with teacher/ peer and discuss how to improve; then re-record.
  • May feel more confident if given chance to rehearse with peer/using tape before speaking to larger group.

Global Rating: (Circle)   lowest 1 ② 3 4 5 highest

ORAL LANGUAGE ASSESSMENT

Reporting on a process

The second text is from Peter, a Polish boy who is twelve years old and in Year 6 at school. Peter arrived in Australia six years ago and speaks only Polish at home. Peter is reporting to the class on an experiment undertaken as part of a group science activity.

P   *Um ... first we have ... we had soil one, soil two, soil three, soil four, soil five. Um, one was peat, soil two ... the sawdust, soil three's um shol ... um potting mix ... mm mixture and der ... we have to ... we had these groups and we had to put 'em and we had ... sunlight, darkness, water ... ten millies of water pool. Water, rain water, tap water and no water and the other group did ... 20 mls of water ... the same as that and ... another group did a ... a fos ... fertilize. Um, the f ... we didn't plant the seeds because of the holidays. We planted the ... the ... ss ... seeds and watered them. We ... um ... had to put three mls because of the week-ends. Um ... some of the ... plants ... the seed already sprouted.*

Oral Language Assessment-REPORTING A PROCESS YEARS 5-6-7

Name of Student: *Peter*   Year Level: *6*   Class: Date:

Task: *Reporting on a science experiment*   Context: *Whole class*

Description of activity: Students share or report on the process they used to complete a task in an individual or group activity.

Criteria (Tick appropriate box)	Very Competent	Competent	Limited Competence	Not Yet	Comments
Ability to carry out the task Did the student:					
• speak appropriately for audience and purpose			✓		*lacked overall clarity*
• complete the task independently, ie with minimal support		✓			*relied on notes*
Structure and Organisation Did the student:					
• set the context; eg "For the plant project we...", "Our experiment was called..."			✓		*insufficient detail – straight into the process*
• provide sufficient detail to convey meaning			✓		
• sequence information, eg "First we did ... , Then we..."			✓		
• stay on the topic		✓			*difficulties within topic*
Language features Did the student:					
• use a range of logical connectives; eg first, then, because, however, although			✓		*and because first*
• use topic-specific vocabulary; eg stiff, beat, beaker, apparatus			✓		*peat, sawdust, sunlight, sprouted*
• use tense, mainly past tense, accurately and consistently; eg "When it was *added*, the mixture *turned* blue and we *concluded* ..."			✓		*use of did + noun (did 20 mls of water)*
• use pronoun reference accurately; eg "We needed *a bunch* of flowers. *It* was supposed to be a huge bunch" not "*They* were supposed to be a huge bunch."			✓		*these groups and we had to put 'em*
Communication skills Did the student:					
• speak fluently without too many hesitations, eg "um"...."er"			✓		*spoke rapidly*
• speak clearly; eg pronounce words accurately, sound plurals and verb endings		✓			*millies*
• self-correct, eg "Then we poured ... sorry, stirred the mixture carefully until ..."		✓			*have → had fos → fertilize*
• refer to the finished product to enhance meaning (optional)					*n/a*

General Comments:
- Peter's report lacked overall clarity. He did not provide a sufficiently detailed context e.g. aim of the experiment and how it was organized (how many groups/what they were to do etc.)
- Moved from one group task to another without clearly establishing what each had done. Ideas introduced but left incomplete.
- Some references unclear e.g. <u>these groups and we had to put 'em</u>
- Lacked specific vocabulary to express ideas concisely.
- Peter needs support in structuring his report eg through focussing questions.
- Could be encouraged to practise using a tape followed by teacher/peer discussion. Needs help with note-making and appropriate use of notes when reporting.

Global Rating: (Circle)   lowest   1   ②   3   4   5   highest

WRITTEN LANGUAGE ASSESSMENT

An argument

The purpose of this task was to write an argument for or against the statement that boys and girls should have separate sports. This text was written by a boy named Tony. Tony was born in Australia and is of Italian background. Both Italian and English are spoken at home. Tony is twelve years old and is in Year 6 at school.

Should girls and boys have separate sports?

one day

The problem is should that boy and girls should have the same sport and then there will be no argument for boy or girls

if girl would play soccer they would look so funny in short and they will probably send the ball of side all of the time and the Ref might get mad all of the time.

but after so many year they have been together they shouldn't be separated and plus some girls think there it and I that those kind of girls because it really get to you and you get so mad and feel like punching them in

The end

Written Language Assessment Activity - ARGUMENT YEARS 5-6-7

Name of Student: _Tony_ Year Level: 6 Class: Date:

Task: _Should girls and boys have separate sports?_ Context: _Unconferenced writing – children to self-edit._

Description of activity: The focus is on justifying a position of interpretation or on arguing that some sort of action be taken. An argument has one line of reasoning or one point of view.

Criteria (Tick appropriate box)	Very Competent	Competent	Limited Competence	Not Yet	Comments
Ability to carry out the task Did the student:			✓		
• write appropriately for audience and purpose					
• complete the task independently, ie with minimal support		✓			_misinterpreted task_
Structure and Organisation Did the student:					_not clear – N.B. use of 'one day'_
• make a position statement			✓		
• present relevant arguments to support position statement			✓		_argues both for and against_
• support the arguments with appropriate evidence			✓		_some evidence unclear_
• show consistency between arguments and the position statement			✓		
• acknowledge or anticipate another viewpoint (optional)			✓		_uses both for & against_
• sum up his/her position consistent with position statement			✓		_'the end'_
• use paragraphs to logically organise arguments		✓			
Language Features Did the student:			✓		_omits plural endings boy/girl_
• use general participants; eg the public, pollution					
• use a range of verbs/processes; eg do, be, have, think			✓		
• use a range of logical connectives: eg			✓		_and, then NB and plus_
- temporal connectives; eg first, next, finally	✓				
- causal connectives; eg therefore, because, so					_because, if_
• use sentence beginnings, ieThemes, that foreground important aspects of the message; ie topic, eg The rainforests ... cause, eg Because of the deforestation, ... time/place, eg In Brazil, ...			✓		_The problem is ... but after so many year..._
• build information about the topic by using nominal groups, eg "The small island state of Tasmania ..."			✓		_the same sport_
• use topic-specific vocabulary appropriately			✓		
• use objective, factual language to persuade or convince the reader			✓		_punching them in / get so mad_
• use passive voice appropriately; eg are required, was used			✓		_be separated_
• use modality; eg may, might, can, could, perhaps, possibly			✓		_should, would, might_
Accuracy Did the student:					
• use grammar accurately: eg					
- tense			✓		
- subject-verb agreement			✓		_it...get_
- reference items; eg this, that, her, who, whose, which			✓		_those kind/ these_
- use accurate syntax (word order); eg words not omitted					
• spell accurately		✓			
• use punctuation accurately		✓			_few capitals, full stops etc._

General Comments: Tony seems to have incorrectly interpreted the task and attempts to argue both for and against the topic. Tries to begin & end the text with a narrative device ie. 'one day' / 'the end'. Mainly uses 'and' to sequence ideas. Attempts the use of modals, but is sometimes inconsistent. Uses inappropriate colloquial expressions eg 'get so mad'. Tony needs support in building and structuring ideas + in choosing appropriate language to express them. Needs practise in linking ideas using a range of connectives. Should be encouraged to self edit his work.

Global Rating: (Circle) lowest 1 ② 3 4 5 highest

I enjoyed the opportunity to work with another teacher in this type of situation — being able to bounce around ideas and thoughts was productive.

(SA Education Dept 1990, p. 14)

This last comment highlights a very important aspect of the procedures: that is, the opportunity they provide for productive interaction between classroom and ESL teachers, either through working collaboratively in planning and carrying out the assessments, or through discussing individual assessments as part of a group moderation process, or through planning teaching strategies and approaches to support children's language development in identified areas of need. In this way the procedures can provide a valuable basis for teachers to evaluate their own work, as well as to gain access to new thinking.

Conclusion

This chapter has outlined an approach to language assessment which has been developed specifically to identify the needs of ESL children in primary classrooms. It has also proved useful in helping teachers to identify what *all* children are able to do in a range of common oral and written learning activities across the curriculum. The information gained through the assessment procedures can be used by teachers at the classroom level in program planning, and at the school level as a basis for reporting on children's progress. The procedures can also provide education authorities with a means of identifying the level of support needed in schools and, in the case of ESL learners, with a measure for the allocation of specialist ESL staffing.

An assessment process which involves teachers in making principled judgments about children's needs in the context of real learning situations provides important opportunities for the re-evaluation of classroom practice. Through using the procedures, teachers have been able to come to a clearer understanding of how language is used to shape meaning in different texts and contexts, and of the ways in which ESL learners can be helped to become successful users of English in the mainstream school situation.

I would like to thank my friends and colleagues at the Languages and Multicultural Unit for their helpful comments on this paper.   L.M.

References

Derewianka, B. 1990, *Exploring How Texts Work*, PETA, Sydney. Distributed by Heinemann.

Gibbons, P. 1991, *Learning to Learn in a Second Language*, PETA, Sydney. Distributed by Heinemann.

Rowe, G. 1989, *Let's Talk: Activities for Oral Language*, Dellasta, Melbourne.

SA Education Dept 1990, ESL Student Needs Assessment Procedures R-10, draft.

Scarino, A., Vale D. & McKay P. 1988, *Australian Language Levels Guidelines*, Curriculum Development Centre, Canberra.

6 THE PRIMARY LANGUAGE RECORD: WHAT WE ARE LEARNING IN THE UK

Myra Barrs

The Primary Language Record is a system of assessing and recording children's development in language and literacy throughout their years of primary schooling. The Record is in two parts: a main (official) record, and an observation and sampling form for teachers' day-to-day recording. The *main record* is meant to be completed at several different points in the school year. It includes the report of a discussion with the child's parents and a language conference held with the child, as well as a summative record of the child's progress and development in English and other community languages. The *observation and samples* form provides two basic structures for keeping track of children's talking and listening, reading and writing: viz. a diary of observations and a range of samples. The informal recording of this form is what the teacher draws on when she comes to complete the main summative record.

The Primary Language Record was developed over an extended period in the last years of the Inner London Education Authority, and has now been in use in some London schools for five years. We are therefore in a good position to evaluate what we are learning from the Record in use and to consider what it is helping teachers to do.

Ever since the Primary Language Record and its accompanying handbook were published in 1988, it has met a remarkable response, both in the UK and in other parts of the world. The Record and handbook have been published in the USA and Canada, teachers in New York and California are taking part in projects to support the use of the Record in their schools, and members of the staff of the Centre for Language in Primary Education (CLPE), where the Record was developed, have visited several countries, including Australia, to talk about it. In the UK the Record has greatly influenced practice in record keeping — an issue currently highlighted as a result of the new national curriculum and its associated system of assessment.

One reason why the Primary Language Record has evoked this kind of response is that it meets a need that has been increasingly felt in a number of different education systems world-wide. This is the need for alternative forms of assessment which will be more informative than conventional assessment, such as standardised tests, and will take into account new approaches to teaching and learning in language and literacy. There have been many important contributions to practice in this area, from miscue analysis in reading to portfolio assessment in writing, but these ways of observing had not previously been combined in any manageable way. The Record offers a synthesis of many exciting practices and incorporates them into a practical classroom record. It draws on work from Australia, Canada, New Zealand and the USA, as well as from the UK, and is a testimony to the existence of a world-wide community of researchers and teachers in the field, many of whom have contributed to these developments.

Paradoxically, moves towards alternative forms of assessment have been taking place in many countries at the same time as the growth of accountability pressures, along with demands for more assessment at every level. The new English national curriculum is a good example of the strength of these pressures for increased measures of accountability. CLPE has recently published *Patterns of Learning* to demonstrate how the Record can be used by teachers to meet the national curriculum criteria for assessment.

Piloting the Primary Language Record

Perhaps the most important aspect of the Primary Language Record is the fact that it has been extensively proved in the classroom. Once it had been drafted by the CLPE-based working party, it was piloted in over fifty schools for nearly a year. Given the speed of more recent developments, that pilot year now seems an immense luxury, but it was an essential factor in adapting the Record to the impress of classroom realities. The schools in the pilot group gave ample feedback about all aspects of the Record, and their comments were fully taken into account in the final draft.

It was also important that the Record was piloted in 'real time' and not just in a quick six-week raid on a few schools. The value of the long pilot time was that as schools became familiar with the Record, their views about some parts of it changed and developed. For instance, at the beginning of the pilot period the general message from the schools was that the discussion with the child's parents, which is the first item on the main record, was far too difficult and time-consuming. It would have to be omitted or made optional. However, towards the end of the period it became apparent that the great majority of the schools had changed their minds about this. The discussions with parents had proved so valuable, and had affected the relationship between homes and schools so profoundly, that most schools were adamant that this element should be retained.

One teacher who took part in the pilot summed up her reaction to the year:

> *Implementing the PLR in its piloting stages was a slow learning process which involved teachers like me volunteering to try it out in our classrooms with advisory support, and attending meetings which involved discussion about our impressions and evaluations. As a result of the trialling, a working party examined the evidence and implemented several changes to make the record a real possibility in a normal busy working day. To use the record effectively meant making some changes in my practice. It meant reassessing the teaching and learning that goes on in class and making time within the day to make observations and record what is actually happening. Although at times it felt like a burden, I felt some ownership and commitment at the end of it and felt that I had moved on in my understanding.*

This teacher pinpoints one of the major outcomes of the Record: its contribution to professional development. Teachers have often emphasised how much they have gained in understanding by using it in the classroom. The question of what teachers have learned and what kind of a contribution the Record can make to teacher education will be discussed later in this chapter.

Since the pilot year, teachers in many schools have helped us to evaluate the Record in use. Advisory teachers concerned with language and literacy across some 800 London schools have conducted evaluations of schools' work with the Record. As one examines this evaluation material, a number of themes emerge.

Themes from evaluation

1 The first year of taking on the Primary Language Record is always a learning year for the schools and teachers involved.

From the very beginning it was emphasised that the introduction of the Record should be seen as a long-term process and should be accompanied by in-service courses and support for schools. Properly used, the Record is not just another set of forms imposed on schools by a central system, but a means of developing work in language and literacy across the curriculum. Teachers are learning new techniques (such as sampling children's reading using a variety of informal methods) and they need time to integrate these into their classroom practice. Sometimes they also need to review their practice — to see how they can make time to observe, for instance, or spend longer periods of time with individual children instead of making more frequent superficial contact.

CLPE staff have now had the experience of introducing the Record to teachers from more than 700 schools through extended in-service courses. A common response at the beginning of such courses is a concern about time, a feeling that the Record is going to be impossible to implement. Keeping detailed observational records of up to thirty children seems just too difficult.

These early reactions are normal and understandable — using the Record does make demands of teachers and of schools. In time, however, and with practice, the concerns die down. The problem arises from teachers feeling that they will be required to implement all elements in the Record, with all children, from the outset. During the course we stress other ways of taking on the Record — observing a small number of children to begin with, or focusing particularly on one aspect of language. Gradually it all comes to seem more manageable. One dramatic shift is illustrated by some comments from the teacher who has already been quoted. In her written evaluation at the beginning of the in-service course in September, she exclaimed:

> *Horrified — completely overwhelmed — when are we going to get time to do it all? Is there going to be any time left for teaching? Is school going to take over my whole life?*

In March of the following year she wrote:

> *As the reading aspect is of particular personal interest, it was most reassuring to find that ideas which I had been working out for myself were being recommended. The PLR is making life much easier.*

It would be untrue to say that all teachers change their views as dramatically as this, but it does seem to be the case that it takes a full school year to 'learn the forms', to internalise the ways of observing that they encapsulate and to see the full value of this kind of recording. Another teacher gave the following advice to teachers new to the Record:

> *Don't panic. Try to think of one area to start from rather than trying to focus on the whole thing. Take one aspect at the beginning — get that firmly in your head. Take it on board in your teaching and your observations and then try a different aspect and add to that.*

2 The in-service accompanying the introduction of the Primary Language Record has been an important factor in its dissemination.

The first courses on the Record were substantial ten-day affairs spread throughout the year. Since then, however, courses have varied from five to eight days, but have never been less than five. This is because they are not just an introduction to the forms, but a thorough course on language and literacy development and informal assessment, dealing with the theoretical structures behind the forms as well as the practical questions of how to use them. Issues such as bilingualism, equal opportunities and special educational needs were fully taken into account in drafting the forms, and so are built into the course.

Teachers who have attended the in-service courses have generally evaluated them positively, stressing how important this kind of support has been in enabling them to use the Record and to introduce it to other colleagues. During the courses some time has been spent in discussing this all-important question of how to share the in-service experience of one or two teachers with the rest of the school staff. Tutors have made course materials available for teachers to take back and work with in their schools. A partner system (whereby each course member pairs up with a staff member back in school) has been encouraged, as well as informal support groups in local areas where course members can continue to meet after their course is over. One teacher described how this support system operated for her:

> *The course was one day a week. I shared my experience of it each week at an informal meeting and I had a 'partner' who tried each school-based activity. Other colleagues became involved on an informal basis. Gradually my negative view changed. The structure and the content of the course gave me confidence ... I am gaining support from ... an excellent advisory teacher who gives positive input, and a coordinators' support group — invaluable for sharing experiences.*

3 Some aspects of the Primary Language Record are taken on more readily than others.

It has become clear that some elements of the Record are soon appreciated by schools, while others take much longer to establish. In general, most schools have endorsed the experience of the pilot group in finding the discussions with the child's parent(s), and the language and literacy conferences with the children themselves, extremely valuable. They have learned so much from these discussions that they consider the time involved well spent. The language and literacy conferences have revealed that children know a great deal about their own learning processes and appreciate being involved in their own assessment.

The reading and writing samples have established themselves quickly in schools because they provide clear structures for analysing what is going on in a piece of writing or during a particular reading occasion. The value of writing down observations within a clear framework has been obvious.

Least fully utilised have been the observation diaries. Because these are such open forms of recording, teachers have not always been able to decide what to record. Those who have worked on this aspect of the Record, however, tend to think that it is one of its most important elements. A head teacher has written:

> *Because of its very abstract nature the talking/listening part of the PLR gave us the greatest anxiety. We are now firmly convinced that this part of the PLR is perhaps the most revealing and vital. The record keeping has made us far more aware of children's reactions and speech in a variety of situations ... Our ears are becoming tuned in to meaningful 'talk' which*

reveals progression and sometimes language problems. We have become much more aware of the importance of the listening skills required of a teacher.

In infant classes the diaries have often proved the most popular part of the Record — teachers of this age group are more used to observation-based recording and to building up a picture of a child's pattern of behaviour over time.

4 The role of the head teacher is vital.

All the evaluation material gathered stresses that the key factor in implementing the Record has been the commitment and support of the head teacher. The amount of discussion time the head is prepared to allow for the introduction of the Record, and to support staff in taking it on, very much affects teachers' readiness to use it. Arranging the discussions between teachers and parents also requires the full backing and organisational skills of the head teacher, and the degree of success in introducing this part of the Record has often affected staff attitudes to implementing the rest of it.

5 The Primary Language Record has helped to improve communications.

One of the main aims in initiating the development of the Record was to improve communications between home and school, and between teachers within the school. This aim seems to have been fulfilled. Most noticeably, the Record has been appreciated by parents, who have welcomed the opportunity to contribute in this way to the school's picture of the child. One teacher, looking back on her own experience, commented:

> *When I first arrived at the school the first year, out of a class of thirty you might get seven, eight, nine parents at the parents' evening and that was all. Now we've introduced the Language Record and we get virtually everybody. I was talking to a parent about it the other day and she said we get a really good response, and I said yes, it's changed. And she said it was because, one, there was really something to discuss, not a fifteen-minute waffle, and also they know now that what they say gets written down.*

Parents have liked having their contributions recorded. It has demonstrated that the school is taking their views seriously and taking them into account in planning and teaching.

The discussion with parents has had particular benefits for bilingual children and their parents. The discussions have done more than anything else to draw attention to the often impressive range of a child's literacies. The record that follows (kindly supplied by Shapla School) demonstrates what has been revealed by asking parents to say more about their children's linguistic achievements.

Part A To be completed during the Autumn Term

A1 Record of discussion between child's parent(s) and class teacher *(Handbook pages 12-13)*

Sumi goes to Arabic school 3 x a week (1¼ hrs. each) where she reads Koran and says namaj. Sumi has Bengali books at home – she reads them with her Mum or Dad or brother Imran. She also brings English books from school and reads them with her family. Sumi has friends near her house but she stays inside and plays with her brothers and likes to help her Mum do housework and cooking. Sumi does lots of writing at home – in English she makes up stories from her head and in Bengali she does practising and she can write in Bengali but not without looking at books. Mum thinks her writing in English is very good and reading (English) not so good but getting better. In Bengali, reading is very good and writing is OK.

Signed Parent(s)___F. K. C._____Teacher___J. W._____

Date___6.10.89_____

Within schools and between schools, the Record has helped to improve the quality of information that teachers are able to give each other. During the first year of implementation some teachers kept evaluation diaries and charted their experience of using the Record. The following entry shows how useful the Record can be at transfer points — either between classes or schools, or, as here, when a teacher takes over a class halfway through the year.

New teacher for the middle infants. The method shows its worth as she can take over a completed parent conference, child conference, reading and writing sample for each child.

At a different level, professional communication within the staff group can be helped by the fact that the Record provides a common language for discussing language, literacy and children's progress. Similarly, the handbook can provide a text for 'shared reading' about language and assessment. The Record emphasises that all teachers who teach the child should contribute to the child's record, and this helps ensure that support teachers, community language teachers, reading teachers and other staff are involved in such discussions.

6 *There is some evidence of improved achievement from schools implementing the Primary Language Record systematically.*

Though it would be hard, perhaps impossible, to support this impression without a careful longitudinal study, it is nevertheless true that many experienced teachers believe that children are benefiting from the use of the Record, and that they have made noticeably more progress in literacy where the Record is systematically used. When discussing this, teachers comment on three factors in particular.

1 The Record provides a structure for teachers and enables them to be more analytical in their observations.

2 As a result, it helps teachers plan the next steps for individuals and the class as a whole. It is true formative assessment which feeds directly into teaching and planning, as the following extract from an evaluation diary shows:

> *I have now completed a reading sample for all my children, plotted them on Reading Scale 1 and used them to plan this term's reading strategies. 16 out of the 26 top infants not yet at point 3 on the scale. More emphasis on reading to try and improve this. Reading samples show quite clearly that some of these are over-reliant on phonics, others on context/memory, others have some grasp of both but are inexperienced. Group work will be aimed specifically at these areas this term.*

3 The involvement of children in the Record, particularly through the language and literacy conference, has been an important development. There is space for children to reflect on their own progress and on their learning processes. The effect of taking children's views seriously in this form of self-assessment has been to engender more positive attitudes.

We hope in time to be able to gather more evidence of the effect of this kind of assessment on children's achievement and teachers' expectations (factors obviously linked), and are beginning with some small-scale research into the use of the reading scales incorporated in the Record.

7 The Primary Language Record has influenced teachers' practice in relation to bilingual children.

As one deputy head commented:

> *Bilingualism is easy to take into account because it's written into [the Record]. It can't be glossed over ... You have to think about the way you teach and then readjust.*

Many elements of the Record reflect its systematic emphasis on the need to be aware of children's bilingualism, and to support the development of their first language(s) as well as English. At each point the teacher is asked to comment on the child's listening, speaking, reading and writing in English and in other community languages. Faced with this regular reminder that children may have linguistic resources that are not being recognised, teachers have typically become more sensitive to issues of bilingualism.

In general, all those involved with the Record have become far more aware of the interrelatedness of languages in bilingual children's development, and of the way in which development in one aspect of language can support development in another. For many teachers this emphasis has helped, more than any other single factor, to dispel the myth of linguistic deprivation which has dogged educational thinking in Britain for so long.

8 Talk has been the most difficult aspect of language to record.

Deciding what to write in the talking and listening diary has been the most challenging task in keeping the Record. However, the mere fact of keeping a record of talk has visibly stimulated practice in this area, and when teachers have focused on keeping the diary, they have been more inclined to create occasions in the classroom during which talk for learning can go on and be encouraged. In-service sessions on talking and listening have frequently led teachers to institute small group work.

Teachers who regularly use the talking and listening diary find that it helps them to keep track of children who might otherwise escape their attention in a busy class. Elizabeth Dawson (1990) has written:

> *I tend to make the most* recorded *observations on those children whose development is slower or less obvious to me. I monitor their oral language development especially carefully in order to gain evidence of their thinking and learning right across the curriculum. I also find it quite easy to record examples of especially skilled use of spoken language. When I have not recorded many observations about a child, use of the diary alerts me to this, so that I am made to consider the reasons why. Is s/he being denied appropriate opportunities for expression? Am I paying her/him a fair amount of attention? Is s/he dominated by others? Is s/he shy with adults?*

Teachers of young and rapidly developing children, or of bilingual children whose development in English they are focusing on, have found this part of the Record particularly valuable. In general, however, recording and assessing talk presents the greatest challenge. It demonstrates more visibly than assessment in any other language mode how far children's development in language is of a piece with the rest of their development (particularly their affective development) and with their relationships.

9 The introduction of the Primary Language Record has strongly supported professional development in language and literacy.

Although, by implication, this point has been made several times already, it does deserve extra emphasis. It has been a key outcome for CLPE staff, who have been centrally involved in the in-service courses associated with the Record, as well as for staff in education offices and schools where it has been introduced. The Record has provided a firm structure for in-service courses and materials, and has proved to be a most effective focus. There can, of course, be no such thing as system development without teacher development. Any system depends on the quality of its teachers. Thus the value of a sound framework for professional development of this kind can be far-reaching.

On many occasions teachers have expressed the increased confidence they feel as a consequence of using the Record — notably in the evaluation reports they complete on CLPE courses. It is in this sense of being more in control of one's work, more confident and informed as a professional, that we see one of the major benefits of the Record. Good informal assessment procedures, like those built into the Record, lead to reflection, and often to changed practice. One teacher, Kathy Gore, who used the Record as a means of observing children for her MA dissertation (a not uncommon use), commented on the process of change she felt she had been involved in. She saw the key change she had made in terms of a move towards greater observation in her teaching — a move that necessitated many other changes.

> *It is in this difficult area of organisation that the real learning often begins. For me it involved a close look [at] and questioning of the value of classroom interactions, the quality of interaction between teacher and children and peer group interaction too. It heightens awareness of the very high quality of children's learning when they are given ownership of it. It encourages teachers to let go a little and allow the children to be more dominant. It involves children in the process and in this way makes learning more open and more easily understood ... In my experience the PLR gives teachers as well as children a new sense of value and competence.*

References

Barrs, M., Ellis. S., Hester, H. & Thomas, A. 1988, *The Primary Language Record: Handbook for Teachers*, Centre for Language in Primary Education, London. Distributed by Heinemann in U.S.A and Pembroke Publishers in Canada.

—— 1990, *Patterns of Learning: The Primary Language Record and the National Curriculum*, Centre for Language in Primary Education, London.

Dawson, E. 1990, 'Sampling talk: An indication of development', *Language Matters,* no. 1, pp. 23-24.

Gore, K. 1990, Reading texts creating worlds: Observing children in the early years, MA dissertation, University of London.

7 ASSESSING STUDENTS' WRITING
a hands-on guide from the Northern Territory

Vivienne Hayward

Teachers' responses to students' writing can be a source of great frustration and mystification. Neither the young writer whose work receives '8/10 – B', nor the one who is told 'A lovely story: you have a great imagination', has been given any guidance about how they are developing as writers. In the first case, it appears that there are some criteria in the teacher's head by which she decides that the writing could have been better (otherwise it would have been given 10/10!), but she is not letting on what they are. In the second case, it is hard to escape thinking that either the teacher believes that warm affection alone will result in the student's growth as a writer, or else that she does not know what she is looking for or what advice to offer. In both cases, the students' growth as autonomous writers and learners is stultified because they have not been given the criteria by which writing is valued in our society.

What tools are needed?

While the assessment of students' writing attainment is only one aspect of their literacy profile, it is an important one. As we have developed our English curriculum in the Northern Territory, we have been very conscious of the need to give students the tools by which they can develop as autonomous writers. We believe that it is really important for teachers, students and parents or care-givers to share understandings of what is involved in measuring student attainment, so that progress can be analysed and decisions taken about what still has to be learnt. In one sense the most important partner in this process is, of course, the student. If students take responsibility for their own education and participate in the decision-making process, it is likely that they will learn effectively. But they can only take on such responsibility if they have an information base from which to work.

There are three parts to this information base, i.e. three sets of things you need to know in order to work out how you are getting on in any learning activity.

1 You need to understand what the activity is and what proficiency in it involves.

2 You need to know the steps along the pathway to proficiency in the activity.

3 You need to know how, in the opinion of the 'expert', you are progressing along this pathway.

For example, if you want to play championship tennis you need to know (1) what the game of tennis is — what you use to play it and what are its rules, (2) what is involved in getting better at it, and (3) whether your coach feels you are at the stage of the beginner's game, the first division or the national side. It is the same with writing: firstly, you need to know what are regarded as the characteristics of proficient writing; secondly, what is involved in developing your writing proficiency, and, thirdly, how you are getting on as a writer.

What are the characteristics of proficient writing?

The characteristics of proficient writing are constant — that is, a narrative is always a narrative, with the same generic features, irrespective of the sophistication with which the writer can handle the genre. A report is a report and so on, just as a game of tennis is a game of tennis irrespective of the skill of the players.

The distinguishing features of a written text, the things that tell us whether it is a recount, a narrative, an argument or an explanation, for example, can easily be identified and used as a basic framework for discussing the success of a piece of student writing.

> *Thus the first tool that teachers, students, parents or care-givers need to assess writing proficiency is a knowledge of the features of the different types of text that occur in written English.*

What stages are there on the developmental pathway towards proficiency in the different kinds of writing?

Teachers' understandings of the steps along the pathway towards writing proficiency are based (implicitly, if not explicitly) on the assumption that from the beginning students will be writing whole texts, and that as they progress along the continuum of learning, they will be gaining increasingly detailed mastery of:

- the features of the genres in which they write

- the language registers and conventions of written expression appropriate to the context in which they are writing

- how to approach a writing task.

For example, a young student's report writing may simply contain a heading and several one-sentence information items about the subject; it may use everyday language, with words spelled as well as the young writer can manage. What the student explicitly knows about 'being a writer' may be that you write down what you know and show it to someone else, who then reads it. But it is more than likely that he or she will have far greater implicit knowledge and can be shown what this is.

On the other hand, a student at the end of primary school may well write a report based on information derived from several sources, beginning with a paragraph delineating the scope of the report, which leads into itemised, detailed information set out in a logical sequence. Technical terms and impersonal language are used where appropriate, and spelling and punctuation are well controlled. This student probably knows explicitly about reading for information, note making, drafting, seeking response and reflecting on the draft, editing, and so on. Again, he or she probably has far more implicit knowledge which can be made explicit.

Thus the second tool needed to assess writing proficiency is a set of benchmarks, or an indication of stages on the developmental pathway towards proficiency in the different kinds of writing.

What do informed and experienced teachers typically expect of students at various stages along the pathway of writing development?

The characteristics (and therefore indications) of various degrees of proficiency can be derived from teachers' experience. The Year 1 teacher sees enough pieces of writing to be confident of knowing the range and kinds of proficiency which can be expected from students at this level. The same is true of the Year 6 teacher, and so on. It is likely, however, that neither will have the same degree of confidence about what is to be expected from each other's classes — never mind what is to be expected of students in Year 10. But since teaching is ideally a collaborative rather than a private task, there is no reason why teachers cannot get together to compile and share samples of student writing. Such a compilation provides indicators of students' writing development for the information and use of all concerned: teachers, students, parents or care-givers.

> *Thus the third tool needed to assess writing proficiency is a set of samples of student writing, ideally annotated to show what they demonstrate about their authors' writing proficiency.*

Developing the tools

Teachers in the Northern Territory, through our Curriculum and Assessment Branch, are in the process of developing and refining these three tools and sharing understandings about how best to use them. Since 1988 we have been producing a series of booklets which teachers can use in schools to help them assess and report on their students' writing.

Under the series title *Primary Assessment Program: Children's Writing in the Northern Territory*, the booklets provide samples of writing by Year 5 and Year 7 students in both urban and Aboriginal schools (and by Year 3 students in Aboriginal schools) in the genres of narrative, report, argument and explanation. Each book is divided into two sections, the first providing information about the genre, the second providing examples of poor, satisfactory and high levels of student writing. Each script is analysed in terms of a predetermined assessment framework, and comments on each are included.

As an example, part of the guidance on assessment of *argument* is reproduced in the following pages. The three samples of Year 7 students' arguments were assessed and then annotated to indicate the reasons why they were valued as they were. The criteria for assessment were those specified in the draft *English Curriculum for Years T–10*, which says that by Year 7:

> *students should demonstrate the beginning ability, based on both primary and secondary sources:*
> *– to argue a case,*
> *– to justify or persuade others to hold a point of view.*
>
> *These argument and persuasion texts should demonstrate students' ability:*
>
> *(a) to use information and data which are sufficient for the purpose, typical of the case being put, i.e. representative of what is known: neither distorting by omission nor arguing on the basis of material unrepresentative of the whole, accurate and relevant,*
>
> *(b) to derive a conclusion logically from the evidence presented,*
>
> *(c) to use the schematic structure appropriate for the genre, and the formalities of particular modes of expression such as the letter and the 'essay',*

(d) to use a register appropriate for the relationship between the writer and the intended audience,

(e) to write at sufficient length to allow all relevant material to be presented in a logical and cohesive manner. By the end of Year 7, students are expected to demonstrate the ability to write at least 250 words of argument or persuasion text.

OBSERVATIONS ON ARGUMENT WRITING SAMPLES

When we talk about argument we don't mean contradicting other people, we mean giving an opinion about the subject backed up with evidence, which we can show justifies our opinion. When we develop an argument we are putting forward a series of reasons why a particular point of view about a subject is justified.

SCHEMATIC STRUCTURE

In the opening paragraph it is usual to state what point of view is being put forward about what subject. It is extremely important that students identify very clearly the exact subject matter being dealt with. This can be defined by stating a question which is to be addressed. Students need to identify very clearly what opinion about the subject they are seeking to justify. For example:

Subject:	Snakes
Thesis or theme 1:	Snakes are dangerous
Thesis or theme 2:	Snakes are fascinating and beautiful
Subject:	My Teacher
Thesis or theme 1:	My teacher is a great person
Thesis or theme 2:	My teacher knows what s/he is talking about

The opinion which the writer seeks to justify about the subject is the theme. The thesis or theme is often re-stated as the conclusion to the argument.

After the opening paragraph the reasons why this point of view is considered justifiable are given. These are the arguments. It is usual to give the argument and then elaborate on it. For example:

Several people die of snake bite in Australia each year.(argument) In 1985 in

Western Australia, the Western Brown killed 3 people and in Queensland in the

same year, the Taipan killed 4.(elaboration)

[Please Note: statistics were created to make the point.]

It is necessary to provide evidence to justify the opinion stated in the argument. This evidence must be factual and as specific as possible. There must be sufficient evidence to support the opinion , i.e., more than one or two facts. The evidence must be 'typical' e.g., if you want to argue about cats using your own cat as a model, you must demonstrate that it is typical of cats.

You must not leave out some significant fact because it doesn't support your argument. Evidence must also be accurate and relevant. The sources of information should be cited and the reason why it should be believed needs to be explained.

Key terms need to be defined. The evidence must be logically sequenced with clear cohesive ties between the steps of the argument. Students need to avoid:

* making overgeneralisations
* making unproved assumptions
* arguing against a person instead of the facts
* misrepresenting a person
* quoting out of context
* using persuasive or emotive language instead of arguing objectively, for example using emotionally loaded nouns, verbs and adjectives. For example, an argument about whether rainforests should be logged should not use expressions such as 'beautiful, cool, shady trees'.

The point of view may be re-stated at the end to sum up the argument. The conclusion must be validly arrived at from the evidence presented in the writing.

LANGUAGE USE/REGISTER

The key features of the way in which language is used in the argument genre are:

* the writer is required to introduce and argue opinion (which may be personal and immature). Such argument must be built upon exposition of relevant facts or information.

* it can be impersonal - does not use first or second person.

* it can be personal (having established the authority base from which to argue opinion) leading to a concluding judgement.

N.B. Besides the 'observations' reproduced above, a series of more detailed notes or 'checklist descriptors' is provided to support the assessment framework shown opposite.

FRAMEWORK FOR ASSESSING ARGUMENT

	Poor	Satis	High
Subject Matter			
1. How clearly does the title indicate the subject or theme?			
2. Is the subject clearly stated?			
3. How clearly is the theme/thesis/proposition stated?			

4. Is the evidence;
 	
     (a) sufficient
 	
     (b) typical
 	
     (c) accurate
 	
     (d) relevant
  To what extent?			

5 . Is the authority of the source stated?			
6. How well are key terms defined?			
Organisation/Generic Structure			
1. How well does the writing follow the structure of an argument?			
2. How well does the opening paragraph state the scope of the argument and the theme/thesis?			
3. How cohesive is the material in each paragraph?			
4. How well used are cohesive links between paragraphs?			
5. How well does the final paragraph conclude the argument?			
Language Use/Register			
1. How appropriate and effective is the vocabulary?			
2. How appropriate is the sentence length and structure?			
3. How consistent is the use of verb tense?			
Care in Presentation			
1. How accurate is the spelling?			
2. How well presented and legible is the handwriting?			
3. How well does the punctuation conform with year level requirements?			
4. How well has the writer acknowledged sources of information?			

"Satisfactory" refers to the general level of writing ability of a student from an English speaking background placed in the context of other students of the same age and the same year of schooling.

BOYS SHOULDN'T CRY

I believe that the statement "Boys shouldn't cry" is unreasonable, unfair and sexist.

Some people say that boys shouldn't cry because it's silly, not masculine, not macho, not tough. But to say that is like saying that there is not a reason for anyone at all to cry. There are many reasons for people to cry. If a person gets hurt emotionally or physically they might want to cry, and it's their right to cry if they want to.

No one is surprised if little children, boys and girls cry. It is a normal reaction, a hormonal function of the human body to physical or emotional distress.

With aging this doesn't change. Tolerance increases, we can bare greater pain and stress so we (men and women) cry less as we get older. But extreme pain e.g. a broken leg or the loss of a loved one will trigger the same reaction to cry. It is unreasonable and unfair to expect men to have greater tolerance than women.

Such an expectation is unhealthy too. People who don't let out their anxiety through crying might build up a stress level in their body and mind. High stress is a basic condition for mental disorders, violence, heart disease and many other physical problems.

①

Crying helps relieve tension and so prevent mental and physical sickness.

Men and boys do cry; it is natural for every human being, it is good to release stress and to reduce pain. It is unrealistic to expect boys not to cry.

BOYS SHOULDN'T CRY

SUBJECT MATTER

* Title clearly indicates the subject.
* The subject is stated very clearly.
* The author's opinion is clearly stated.
* Several pieces of evidence have been provided. They are typical, accurate, relevant and of a high quality.
* Sources have not been stated.
* Some of the key terms have been defined.
* The author has attempted to select the salient points of each paragraph and draw these together as a conclusion.

ORGANISATION/GENERIC STRUCTURE

* The text follows the structure of an argument.
* The scope of the argument is quite well developed in the first paragraph. The mechanics used to construct the argument are very good.
* New ideas are consistently awarded new paragraphs.
* Cohesive links between paragraphs are very good.
* Final paragraph is validly derived from the evidence presented.

LANGUAGE USE/REGISTER

* The use of vocabulary is appropriate and effective. The author shows particularly good use of abstractions and generalisations.
* A range of sentence structures and lengths has been used.

CARE IN PRESENTATION

* Spelling is good, although some minor errors are in evidence.
* Handwriting is well presented and legible.
* Punctuation is consistent. The author uses a semi colon effectively, though a colon would have been better.
* No sources have been included.

YEAR 7 ARGUMENT HIGH STANDARD

Should Children Receive Pocket Money?

I think kids should get some sort of pocket money even if it is only $1 a week. Sometimes kids want to go out and muck around with his or her friend. Kids sometimes get bored at home and want to go to a video game shop to play games. They advertise about how kids should come in and have fun for only $5. Parents think its a great idea and pretty cheap to. So kids can use their pocket money instead of asking their parents every 5 minutes for pocket money.

Kids also need money to pay for sports such as indoor cricket where you have to pay weekly or soccer where you have to pay money at the start of the season. Kids like to play sports and parents encourage them to play but like most things in the world you have to pay money for it. Some kids are lucky enough to play for town, city, state or territory sides for sport which also envolves money.

Kids need money to buy things for Motherday, Fatherzday, Birthdays, Christmas and Easter. How do parents expect them to buy these things without pocket money. Kids have got great ideas for Mums and Dads and brothers and sisters presents but no money to buy them with. Kids like to buy their Mum things like chocolate, flowers, little gimmicks and so on. Kids like to receive but also give.

Kids like to buy things for school. Like little rubbers in the shape of an animal or a gun. They like to buy things like coloured pens, pencils, ink, textas and so on. They buy things that doesn't cost alot of money.

People may disagree but the kids are happy and they still have enough change to buy a lollie with the 60 change. So thats why I think kids should get pocket money.

SHOULD CHILDREN RECEIVE POCKET MONEY?

SUBJECT MATTER

* Title clearly indicates subject.
* Subject is clearly stated.
* The author's opinion is clear.
* All the evidence included is the author's opinion. All evidence is based on one level - 'kids need money for...' - a statement of wants, not needs. The evidence is not typical and not all is relevant.
* All evidence included is the author's opinion.
* Key terms have not been defined, for example receive (gift? or earning?), children.
* The conclusion flows well but the argument is circular.

ORGANISATION/GENERIC STRUCTURE

* Opening paragraph begins to define the scope.
* Paragraphs are used well, with each new facet of the argument appearing in a new paragraph.
* Cohesive links are included.
* Conclusion is weak.

LANGUAGE USE/REGISTER

* Colloquial language is used, for example 'kids' and 'muck around' in what is essentially a formal argument.
* The author is attempting to use complex sentences, with varying success.

CARE IN PRESENTATION

* Spelling is satisfactory: although there are errors, they do not interrupt the reader's ability to follow the argument.
* Handwriting is neat and legible.
* Punctuation is satisfactory. The author has omitted question marks on some occasions and apostrophe in that's.
* No sources were quoted; personal opinion only.

YEAR 7 ARGUMENT SATISFACTORY STANDARD

Ban R-Rated Movies

I wish that R-rated movies would be banned, because they are dirty horrble and disgusting for younger people if they watch them.

The survey on the bottom of the page will show you how many people want to watch R-rated movies and how many people don't want to watch R-rated movies. Out of two typical Darwn families my brathers watched one but they didn't like it and they returnd it to the video shop beccuse it had to mech violent. Then they got another one but that was even more violent so they took that back as well.

I don't know why it is necessary for R-rated moives to be made in the fists place.

Yes	No
	✓✓✓✓✓✓✓✓

All of the answers wanted more control or more suppervision at the vido shops.

BAN R-RATED MOVIES

SUBJECT MATTER

* Title is an instruction. A more appropriate title for an argument might be 'R rated movies should be banned'.
* The subject and theme are clearly stated.
* The writer is aware of the role of opinion polls and has used one to substantiate personal opinion. The evidence tendered is based on the author's opinion and the opinions of 2 brothers and 8 peers, not necessarily representative of the wider group. Much evidence has been omitted. Included evidence is relevant.
* Sources are stated, 2 brothers and 8 peers, but the scope is not adequate.
* Key terms are not defined.
* Conclusion flows from the body of the passage.
* This passage is too short - 130 words is not acceptable for a Year 7 text. Conferencing might have developed this piece further.

ORGANISATION/GENERIC STRUCTURE

* Paragraph 1 states the scope of the argument.
* Paragraph structure is poor.
* Cohesive links are not evident.

LANGUAGE USE/REGISTER

* The author's vocabulary is satisfactory.
* Sentence structure and sentence length are satisfactory. Passage includes complex sentences.

CARE IN PRESENTATION

* Mastery of spelling is poor.
* Printing is not appropriate at Year 7 level.
* Punctuation is consistent with Year 7 requirements.
* Sources of information have been noted.

YEAR 7 ARGUMENT POOR STANDARD

What are the benefits?

With the *Primary Assessment Program*, then, teachers and schools in the Northern Territory have access to knowledge of the features of different types of text that occur in written English, a set of benchmarks or an indication (in the draft *English Curriculum*) of stages on the developmental pathway towards proficiency in each kind of writing, and a set of written samples annotated to show what they demonstrate about their authors' writing proficiency.

Individual teachers can use these three sets of information tools:

- to develop their own understandings about writing, which they can make explicit for students, parents or care-givers, and use in their own teaching

- as a guide for assessing their students' writing, and to give students a means of assessing their own writing

- as a basis for reporting to parents or care-givers.

School communities can use them to:

- develop their own set of samples of student writing, derived from their own context

- develop common understandings about the teaching of writing throughout the school

- help in the development of their school's assessment policy and strategies, and as the basis of inter-class and inter-year moderation

- help in the framing of their reporting policy.

There are several advantages in this approach to assessment. Unlike standardised tests, it acknowledges that students should be assessed on their attainments in specific classroom contexts and specific learning tasks. At the same time, it provides a common framework and standard which teachers can use to assess and report on their students' attainments, confident that they are doing so according to criteria and standards agreed to by other informed and experienced teachers. It makes these criteria and standards explicit for all involved, which is not only a matter of natural justice, but also a powerful means of enabling students to know how they may grow as writers. This in turn contributes to their capacity to become autonomous learners — the ultimate goal of all our efforts as teachers.

References

Northern Territory Department of Education 1990a, *Moderated Examples of Argument and Explanation from Year 5 and Year 7*, Primary Assessment Program: Children's Writing in the Northern Territory, Darwin.

—— 1990b, *The English Curriculum for Years T–10*, draft.

8 ARE PROFILES ENOUGH?

Chrystine Bouffler

Earlier in this book (pp. 34-36) John Dwyer has described the nature and development of the Victorian *Literacy Profiles*. It is argued by those responsible for them that they are attractive for a number of reasons: they describe students' literacy behaviour in terms of teacher-researched criteria, they are analytical and so can be used for diagnostic purposes, and they can track the gradual emergence of students' literacy competencies. At a general level the claims are probably justified. However, whether they are analytical and diagnostic enough to meet the needs of the classroom teacher is a matter of debate. Certainly there is a danger of falling into the very traps the profiles were designed to avoid unless teachers operate from a clearly articulated theory of language which includes consistent theories of reading and writing.

It seems to me that if the profiles are not informed by a theoretical stance, they can easily become no more than a checklist of literacy behaviours, diagnostic only in so far as they reveal gaps in student behaviour. This may be all the information the system requires, but a teacher needs information on the quality of students' responses and an indication of how any problems might be solved. And it is your theoretical stance which enables you to recognise significant literacy behaviour and then to make judgements about it.

For the purposes of illustration I will confine discussion in this chapter to the area of reading. No clear theory of reading underpins the profiles (although a brief statement of a 'philosophical base' is included in the Handbook). Rather there appear to be elements of several theories in the indicators listed, some of which focus on prediction and the use of context cues, while others suggest a concern for word-based reading strategies. This lack of clear theoretical definition is not surprising given that the profiles were developed by a number of

---

READING BAND   B   ☐

Reading Strategies   ☐──────────────────────────────────

Takes risks when reading.

"Reads" books with simple repetitive language patterns.

Uses pictures for clues to meaning of text.

Asks others for help with meaning and pronunciation of words.

Consistently reads familiar words and interprets symbols within a text.

Predicts words.

Matches known clusters of letters to clusters in unknown words.

Uses knowledge of words in the environment when "reading" and "writing".

Recognises base words within other words.

Names basic parts of a book.

Makes a second attempt at a word if it doesn't sound right.

Responses   ☐──────────────────────────────────

Selects own books to "read".

Describes connections among events in texts.

Writes, role plays and/or draws in response to a story or other form of writing
    (e.g. poem, message).

Creates ending when the text is left unfinished.

Recounts parts of text in writing, drama, or art work.

Retells using language expressions from reading sources.

Retells with approximate sequence.

A sample of indicators

teachers, amongst whom there was no doubt a fair degree of theoretical variation.

Reference to the Victorian curriculum statement *The English Language Framework P-10* is somewhat more illuminating in that it does provide a theoretical stance in defining reading (p. 22), although inevitably in such a document there is little elaboration. The contexts for observing behaviours associated with each band in the *Profiles* Handbook suggest that the theory adopted in the *Framework* statement is the one that should underpin the profiles, but the extent to which it does will depend largely on the interpretations of teachers who use them. Essentially this theory is the one proposed by Goodman (1967) and Smith (1988), who drew on extensive research in language and psychology. They consider reading a process which involves the reader in scanning the print, predicting meaning, and confirming or correcting the predictions on the basis of continued scanning. The creation of meaning is the driving force for this process.

In order to predict the reader makes use of prior knowledge, which includes a general knowledge of how things are in the world and a more specific knowledge of language. The latter involves knowledge of the cue systems, i.e. the semantic or meaning system, the syntactic or grammar system, and the graphophonic or sound-symbol system. The theory sees reading as a holistic process of making meaning that cannot be divided into sets of discrete skills.

Most teachers to-day are familiar with this theory, though not necessarily with its relationship to a general theory of language and its implications for classroom practice. It is consistent with a theory of language which emphasises meaning and strongly asserts that the cue systems of language, whether oral or written, are always present and working together in any instance of language use. Language exists only in a context and these contexts are crucial to making meaning. Since the cue systems of language are always present and working together in any context, it is learned holistically. This is the basis of Whole Language. Unfortunately it is impossible to explore the ramifications of the theory any further within this chapter.

Since teachers with a well-developed theory know what to look for in their students' reading behaviour, it might be said that having a well-developed, well-articulated theory of reading and language makes profiling largely redundant — except that the profiles provide some uniformity of reporting across the system. However, there is anecdotal evidence from teachers that profiles reveal gaps in language learning that were not immediately evident even to teachers with a sound theoretical knowledge. None the less, as I have suggested, the analytic and diagnostic characteristics of the profiles seldom go beyond identifying gaps. Knowing that a child is having difficulty is only the first step. The questions which follow are perhaps more important — what kind of difficulty and why? It is in answering such questions that a teacher requires a theoretical knowledge of language as well as a knowledge of the child. A consideration of the activities recommended in the Handbook's list of contexts for observing reading behaviours across the reading bands (pp. 60-62) will illustrate this. The list is as follows:

Reading conference	Reading logs and journals
Shared reading	Retelling
Quiet reading time	Reading circles and sharing times
Discussions with parents	Readers' theatre
Writing sessions	Miscue analysis
Running records	Observations and anecdotal records
Sand and *Stones* test	Sequencing
Drama and role play	Folios
Cloze activities	Preview activities
Possible sentences	Three level guides
Close analysis	

Each activity is accompanied by a brief description (3-5 lines) and a reference for further reading (mostly to Victorian Ministry publications). It is impossible to cover the whole list here and so I have been selective.

Three types of information can be gathered by observing the activities: how readers process text, how they respond to text, and their attitudes to reading. Retelling, miscue analysis and cloze activities reveal information about processing.

Retelling

At one level a *retelling* can indicate whether a student has understood a particular text or not. The language of the retelling can also indicate how well the reader is able not only to understand but to use the language of books. The profiles will show up difficulties in understanding, but not the reasons for them. There may be two reasons for a lack of understanding.

1 The text selected was beyond the experience of the reader. This tends to be associated with one-off reading situations or a variety of texts related to the one subject. It is unlikely that a student will have this difficulty constantly over a range of reading material.

2 The reader did not have the processing strategies to 'unlock' the text. In this situation it is not so much a matter of whether the text could be retold as of how it was retold. A competent reader will retell a text with little prompting. A less competent reader may require many prompts to achieve a retelling. If a reader needs more than two or three prompts to achieve a reasonable retelling (and has no physical or psychological impairment), then I would suggest that he or she is having trouble storing the overall text out-line in long-term memory. One reason for this happening is that the reader is focusing too much on smaller units of language and predicting at the word, phrase or sentence level only. This can occur when the reader is focusing on sounding out unknown words or reading sentence by sentence, thus over-loading the memory and creating what is known as tunnel vision (Smith 1988, p. 72). In such cases the reader must be helped to use a variety of language cues and to predict beyond the sentence level.

For further information on retelling as a learning/teaching strategy, see *Read and Retell* (Brown & Cambourne 1987).

Miscue analysis and running records

A retelling will alert you to the possibility of processing problems, but further investigation will be needed to confirm them. The most appropriate activity would be some form of *miscue analysis*. Although Clay's *running record* may be considered a form of miscue analysis, it differs considerably from the Goodman, Watson and Burke *reading miscue inventory* in its mode of analysis. While both rely on oral reading, the running record is particularly concerned with accuracy (which I would argue reflects a skills-based view of reading). The reading miscue inventory was initially developed as a research tool and is probably too detailed for general classroom use, but simplified versions are available (e.g. Brennan 1980). The miscue inventory looks at how meaning is maintained at the text, sentence or phrase level, at self-correction, and at the grammatical, phonic or graphic similarity of the reader's miscues to the original text. An oral reading of the text is always followed by a retelling. It is possible for a reader, perhaps through lack of confidence in reading aloud, to have a large number of miscues but to understand what is read. A retelling can also confirm patterns revealed by the miscue analysis.

A miscue analysis is predicated on a particular view of reading and is of little or no value to the teacher who does not share this view. For those who do, it will indicate how a reader is processing text. Self-correction behaviour shows whether a reader is monitoring meaning. All readers miscue, but the miscues are of concern only if they lose meaning and are not corrected. Failure to correct when a miscue loses meaning suggests that the reader is not monitoring what is being read. In this case it is important to establish at what level the meaning is being lost. If the miscue makes sense in the phrase or sentence but not at the text level, and this pattern is repeated, then there is a strong likelihood that the reader is focusing too much on small chunks of texts to the detriment of the total meaning. If this pattern were supported by one which suggested that a large number of miscues were graphically or phonically similar to the word in the text, you could reasonably assume that the reader is over-reliant on graphic and phonic strategies, i.e. making too little use of semantic and syntactic information.

For those who wish to pursue miscue analysis further, a good introduction is to be found in the *Reading Appraisal Guide* (Johnson 1979) and a more detailed examination in *Reading Miscue Inventory: Alternative Procedures* (Goodman, Watson & Burke 1987). Information on running records is to be found in *The Early Detection of Reading Difficulties* (Clay 1985).

Cloze

Given the same theoretical framework, a properly constructed *cloze activity* can reveal information similar to a retelling or miscue analysis. The way readers fill the gaps during silent reading can be judged according to meaning and grammaticality in much the same way as miscues during oral reading. However, the most informative aspect of a cloze activity is not so much its completion as the discussion which may go on during or after it. This provides insights into how readers arrive at their solutions and can reveal information about their use of processing strategies, such as forwards and backwards referencing. Some readers, for instance, will read back to help them fill the gap, but will not read forwards.

In addition, cloze can often reveal knowledge of syntax and, particularly, of book language and idioms, as well as an understanding of stylistic devices. I am put in mind of one cloze discussion which centred around the phrase *but there was none. None* was deleted. The structure was not familiar to the young readers, and although it was obvious that they understood the underlying meaning (since they tried to change the phrase to *there wasn't any*), they were unable to come up with a word for the gap, thus revealing to the teacher their lack of knowledge of this particular kind of structure, which is essentially part of book language.

For further information on cloze, see Unsworth 1985. For information on ways to construct cloze activities for specific teaching and learning purposes, see Parker & Unsworth 1986.

Reader responses

Other listed activities deal with student responses. Understanding readers' responses to texts also requires a theoretical perspective. Since readers do not all bring the same experiences to a text, it is to be expected that they will take different things from it. *Reading conferences, reading circles* and the like can reveal these differences in interpretation, but in order to make judgements about such differences teachers need a sound knowledge of literature and text structure. This involves something more than simply being familiar with a wide range of children's books. You have to know what constitutes good literature, the important elements of different texts, and how they are structured to convey their meaning. This kind of knowledge becomes increasingly important in higher grades.

The indicators for Band E provide a good example of the kind of understanding teachers require.

READING BAND   E   ☐

Reading Strategies ☐ ——————————————————————————————
Reads to others with few inappropriate pauses.
Interprets new words by reference to suffixes, prefixes and meaning of word
  parts.
Uses directories such as a table of contents or index, telephone and street
  directories to locate information.
Uses library classification systems to find specific reading materials.

Responses ☐ ——————————————————————————————————
Improvises in role play, drawing on a range of text.
Writing shows meaning inferred from the text.
Explains a piece of literature.
Expresses and supports an opinion on whether an author's point of view is valid.
Discusses implied motives of characters in the text.
Makes comments and expresses feelings about characters.
Rewrites information from text in own words.
Uses text as a model for own writing.
Uses a range of books and print materials as information sources for written
  work.
Reads aloud with expression.

What might be involved in explaining a piece of literature? Literature operates on a number of levels. From one viewpoint, there is the literal level, which is simply what the story is about, the higher order interpretative level and, one could add, the level of generalisation — the extent to which the message of the text has applications beyond its situation. An explanation in these terms would certainly go beyond mere retelling. From another viewpoint, readers might explain the text in terms of the way the author has chosen to tell the story: for instance, whether a first or third person narrator has been chosen, and how this choice affects the reader's response to the central character.

Knowledge of the way text is structured is also important if *sequencing* is to be a useful observational tool. Before students can sequence stories, the texts must be cut up at appropriate transition points. This assumes that teachers have a general understanding how cohesion is achieved in text and are able to recognise the transition points.

What *quiet reading time* can reveal about readers is discussed in the chapter by Hancock which follows, and there is a wealth of material available on the subject of children's literature. *How Texts Teach What Readers Learn* (Meek 1988), though short, offers an unusually penetrating insight into children's responses. Another useful source of information is *Developing Response to Fiction* (Protherough 1983).

Conclusion

The aim of this chapter has been to demonstrate that an effective use of the Victorian *Literacy Profiles* requires a sound theoretical knowledge. I have used the Victorian situation only as an example; the argument holds true for any kind of assessment. Implicit in the argument is my belief that assessment should not only highlight current strengths and weaknesses in learning but provide a basis for further learning. It must enable the teacher to identify the particular nature of the problem and point up possible solutions. This, after all, is what teaching is about: helping learners to learn. A system-wide form of assessment can scarcely hope to do this unless it is based on a clearly articulated theory and its theoretical perspective is shared by those who use it.

References

Brennan, M. 1980, *BRIM Manual*, Riverina CAE [now Charles Sturt University], Wagga Wagga.

Brown, H. & Cambourne, B. 1987, *Read and Retell*, Methuen, Sydney. Distributed by Heinemann

Clay, M. 1972, *Reading: The Patterning of Complex Behaviour*, Heinemann, Auckland.

—— 1985, *The Early Detection of Reading Difficulties,* 3rd edn, Heinemann, Auckland.

Goodman, K. 1967, 'Reading: A psycholinguistic guessing game', *Journal of the Reading Specialist,* vol. 6, pp. 126-35.

Goodman, Y., Watson, D. & Burke, C. 1987, *Reading Miscue Inventory: Alternative Procedures,* Owen, New York.

Johnson, B. 1979, *Reading Appraisal Guide*, ACER, Melbourne.

Meek, M. 1988, *How Texts Teach What Readers Learn*, Thimble Press, Stroud, Glos., (Included in *The Word for Teaching is Learning*, edited by Martin Lightfoot and Nancy Martin, Heinemann Boyton/Cook, Portsmouth, NH.

Parker, R. & Unsworth, L. 1986, *Bridging the Gaps*, Martin Educational in assoc. with Robert Andersen and Associates, Sydney.

Protherough, R. 1983, *Developing Response to Fiction*, Open University Press, Milton Keynes.

Schools Program Division, Victorian Ministry of Education 1988, *The English Language Framework P-10,* The Education Shop, Melbourne.

—— 1990a, *Literacy Profiles Handbook: Assessing and Reporting Literacy Development*, The Education Shop, Melbourne.

—— 1990b, *Literacy Profiles Manual for Consultants: A Resource Booklet,* The Education Shop, Melbourne.

Smith F. 1988, *Understanding Reading*, 4th edn, Laurence Erlbaum Associates, New Jersey.

Unsworth, L. 1985, 'Cloze procedure applications to assessment in silent reading', in *Reading: An Australian Perspective*, ed. L. Unsworth, Nelson, Melbourne.

9 SIDE-BY-SIDE: RESPONSIVE EVALUATION IN A YEAR FIVE CLASSROOM

Jan Hancock

The ultimate Latin root of *assessment* is *assidere* meaning 'to sit beside'. To view assessment in this light opens a fresh perspective on the evaluation of learning. Rowntree (1977, p. 4) explains that such a description leads to assessment being thought of

> *as occurring whenever one person, in some kind of interaction, direct or indirect, with another, is conscious of obtaining and interpreting information about the knowledge and understandings, or abilities and attitudes of that other person. To some extent or other it is an attempt to know that person.*

This description is congruent with a wholistic approach to teaching and learning, and, more particularly, with the approach I have adopted as a teacher-researcher (Hancock 1991) — one which underpinned the inquiry I carried out into the assessment and evaluation of silent reading in my classroom.

That ubiquitous reading activity, Sustained Silent Reading (SSR), was one of the central features of my instructional practice, and so its assessment seemed imperative. In my classroom, as in most others, SSR involved a set time each day when every student read self-chosen texts silently for a sustained period. I held a strong belief that SSR provided opportunities for widening the experiential base upon which readers draw to understand any texts they encounter. I valued the provision of regular periods of reading within an environment that offered a wide and interesting array of texts matching the experiences of the readers. Equally, I valued the fact that readers could choose their own texts and had opportunities to share and discuss the meanings they gained from them.

I also believed that any assessment of students' growth and development directed at improving language teaching and learning needed to match the understandings I held about how literacy is learned. These understandings and their influence on my assessment techniques are outlined below.

Literacy is learned under collaborative and interactive conditions.
Thus I needed to devise a means of monitoring the degree of engagement or non-engagement via responses to reading that occurred under these conditions.

Literacy is learned with the support of 'real' resources (texts) and 'real' purposes, and with 'real' models or demonstrations.
Thus I needed to devise a means of monitoring the degree of engagement or non-engagement with texts read via responses to the demonstrations and models provided and the purposes to which the reading was directed.

Literacy is learned in conditions that value approximations and the construction of personal representations under non-risk conditions, and that allow reflection on these approximations and representations.
Thus I needed to devise a means of monitoring the degree of engagement or non-engagement via responses to the use of approximations and the construction of personal representations as learning tools, and via responses to reflective questions such as *Why did you do it that way?*, *Did it work for me?* and *How can I do it better?*

The classroom context

The classroom was stocked with 'trade books', i.e. not with reading schemes but with books such as might be found on library shelves. The supply of books varied, with new titles being introduced every five weeks or so. Both the students and I would select titles from the library. Previous experience at this grade level had given me a knowledge of the type of texts suited to the students' interest and reading experience. As the year progressed, the span of texts, both reader-friendly and reader-challenging, grew to cater for all rates of development.

Assessment of the silent reading periods was shared between myself and the students. For me, it involved anecdotal records, a daily survey of reading patterns in the class and a collaborative (teacher and student) evaluation. For the students, it involved recorded reflections on their reading at intervals of three to four weeks, records of their daily reading choices, reading log responses and the collaborative evaluation. I considered that the decisions the students made during SSR reflected their reading proficiency, and so I was confident that monitoring the types of text they chose to read, the periods of time they spent engaged with them and their demonstrated interactions offered a reliable means of responding to their learning processes.

The means of assessment

1 Anecdotal records

Below are examples of anecdotal records that trace the responses of Joseph and Dallas in silent reading periods over several weeks.

JOSEPH

NON-ENGAGEMENT RESPONSES	ENGAGEMENT RESPONSES

T1 Wk 4 *Tuesday*
In SSR very dependent on short reading texts such as poetry books that don't require a sustained period of engagement or demand his concentration.

T1 Wk 5 *Monday*
He selected a fiction book for the first time this year. He needed reassurance that it was a good book before he began.

Tuesday
Still settled with the text 'Charlotte's Web'.

T2 Wk 9 *Monday*
Reads non-fiction text most of the time; he has been reading a rather complex book on the world's inventions. I know he is interested in this topic, but whilst taking the survey today he said to me, 'Miss I don't want to finish this.' I felt that he may have thought all non-fiction books should be read from cover to cover. I took the opportunity later to speak to the whole class and explained that most readers tended to read selections from non-fiction depending on what they were interested in. As they usually have no story or 'plot', there wasn't any need to read all of it.

Tuesday
Maybe he got the message for he is now considering whether he should keep reading it. He decided not to and I said 'That's okay Joseph.'

DALLAS

NON-ENGAGEMENT RESPONSES	ENGAGEMENT RESPONSES

T1 Wk 7 *Monday*
Chopping and changing – said he finished 'Thing' but I'll have to check his comprehension by listening to him read, monitoring miscues, and have him orally retell some of the story tomorrow. Chosen a Joke book.

NON-ENGAGEMENT RESPONSES	ENGAGEMENT RESPONSES

NON-ENGAGEMENT RESPONSES

Tuesday
Not settled with text 'Trailbikes' – distracting Matt and Aaron at the same table.

Wednesday
Still changing every day – reading poetry and non-fiction. Changes text a few times during one session.

Tuesday
Seemed uninterested in the story he was reading out of Paul Jennings' 'Unbelievable'. I was disappointed and showed my surprise that he should be 'bored' with 'Cow Dung Custard' that he was halfway through and had showed so much interest in yesterday. I sat with him and read him the next few episodes of the story (he followed along with me as I read) just to whet his appetite again. This worked to some extent as he got back into it.

ENGAGEMENT RESPONSES

Thursday
Chose a Picture Book – I decided to hear him read it aloud. We read it together in that I read the refrain – I told him it was one of my favourites ('Tailypo') – this allowed me to hear his miscues. Discovered that in the main he reads for meaning and employs some good strategies. However, allows incomprehensible phrases to go by in order 'to get on with it'. We both enjoyed reading together and I realised some of his strengths. He just needs to read more texts that match his experience in reading.

T2 Wk 8 *Monday*
Enjoying the short story fiction; it is not uncommon for him to stop and share bits of them with his neighbour Mark, who always reads well in SR and who has just completed 'Closer to the Stars' and is now reading Aidan Chambers' 'Shades of Dark'. Mark is very interested in Dallas' opinions of the book as it was Mark who encouraged Dallas to read the book in the first place.

Wednesday
Finished 'Cow Dung Custard' and shared it with the class, although the retelling was somewhat confused towards the end. Mark his neighbour is reading 'The Killer Tadpole'. Dallas asked him 'What's it like?' – seemed to ask in a manner that meant 'I might read that next.' I sense his growing interest in reading, I feel the hooks are taking hold – a breakthrough – but I realise from past experience that this pattern of reading will revert to his old pattern, though the chances of change are more likely now.

Over time these records began to build towards a profile of the reader. When they were combined and interpreted with data gathered from the reading survey and collaborative evaluation, what emerged was, in my view, an authentic evaluation of each learner.

2 Teacher reading survey/student reading records

At the beginning of SSR each day I would quietly and systematically carry out a survey by going around the classroom and asking what texts the students had chosen to read. For their part, the students were responsible for recording each new title on a library card, together with the dates they began and finished it. If they chose not to finish a book, they would enter a dash instead.

I recorded the title and type of text on a survey sheet, using the following code: F – fiction, NF – non-fiction, P – poetry, PB – picture book, SSF – short story fiction, CYO – choose your own adventure (see specimen below). If students were reading the same text as the previous day, I did not disturb them but entered an 'S' for 'same'. When a student had chosen a new text, I would ask if the previous one had been finished, and if it had been, that day was marked with a small black square. My decision as to whether students had actually completed a text with adequate comprehension was based on other observations and interactions (retellings, miscue analysis and discussion). I would not record the text as completed if these observations and interactions indicated that the student had not truly engaged with the text.

■ Completed Wk 1	MON	TUES	WED	THUR	FRI
Dallas	North of Danger (F)	S	Papio (F)	S	Kid's Zone (N.F)
Lyn	Are You There God (F)	S	S	S	S
Kellie	Sister Madge (P)	S	Kid Power (F)	Babysitter's Club (F)	S

The criteria used to interpret the data gathered from the survey were these:

- whether the student completed the text with substantial evidence of comprehension

- the length of time spent with the text

- a consistent, settled pattern of selection (not constantly changing)

- a balanced choice of fiction and non-fiction.

The daily survey gave me an opportunity to interact with any of the students. This might take the form of listening to them quietly read small segments of their chosen books, during which I would carry out a mental miscue analysis. I was very familiar with miscue analysis procedures (Goodman, Watson & Burke 1987) and felt confident of 'mentally' rather than 'manually' processing the data. When listening to students read, I demonstrated that they were reading *to* me, not *for* me. I concentrated on meaning. I would say such things as, 'I didn't catch that — what did you say?' or, 'I'm lost there. Could you read that again please?' I wanted them to feel that they were responsible for getting their own meaning from the text. This form of interaction took place when I observed that a student was not engaging with a book. Students picked up on these cues too, for Dallas remarked in a reflection later in the year: *If Miss H. comes over and asks you to read to her I think she doesn't think you're going good.*

Other interactions might involve listening to retellings between neighbours, which took place during 'sharing time' following SSR. Sometimes I might request a brief retelling from individuals as I recorded survey details. Such occasions provided opportunities to enhance students' engagement in reading. If they requested it, I would direct them to texts more suited to their experience. If I found a student continually reading the same type of text (e.g. children's magazines, Choose Your Own Adventure), or if I had noted any unsettled reading, I would suggest a different direction.

Joseph's patterns

For the first four weeks of the year Joseph's preference was for non-fiction, followed by poetry, but at the beginning of Week 5 he chose a fiction book for the first time. It was *Charlotte's Web* by E. B. White, and he slowly but steadily completed it over the next three weeks. He then read a selection of picture books and poetry and revisited a non-fiction text (but did not engage well with it). This pattern of easier reading after a prolonged stretch with fiction was one I saw repeated frequently by other readers.

In Term 2 Joseph returned to non-fiction and was well engaged with a book on robots for four weeks. He read it from cover to cover. In Week 5 he began *The Great Inventions*, another non-fiction text, but although he seemed well engaged again, I was concerned that he was getting bogged down. So I discussed with the whole class the manner in which readers commonly dip into non-fiction texts, in the hope that he would become aware that reading through to completion is not necessarily the way to treat such texts.

Perhaps Joseph took heed of this advice, for his pattern slowly began to change. By Week 9 he had persevered for seven days with a fiction text, though he left it unfinished. Interventions on my part to foster a deeper engagement with fiction consisted of responses to his log book entries, suggestions of fiction texts on the collaborative evaluation sheet and regular verbal encouragement to dip into a variety of text types. At first the suggestions I made did not suit his interests (as his log book entries confirmed), and he spent the last week of the term reading picture books, poetry and Choose Your Own Adventure texts. However, mainly through the retellings of his peers, Joseph was alerted to fiction that interested him more, and this was reflected in his choices. Titles to his liking were those of Roald Dahl and the short stories of Paul Jennings. Joseph's engagement with fiction increased to the extent of his establishing a predominantly fictional diet by the end of Term 3. This continued through Term 4, as the following graph shows.

JOSEPH'S SILENT READING RECORD

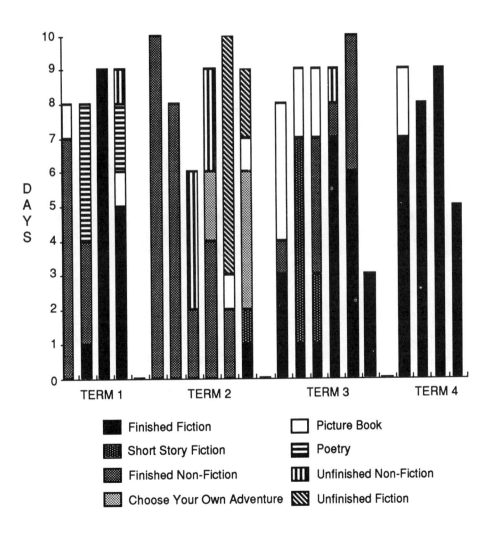

Dallas' patterns

Dallas revealed very different patterns. At the beginning of the year he appeared to have some difficulty in settling on a suitable text. By the end of the first four weeks he had only engaged well with three texts, none of which involved him in any sustained reading. I had intervened on numerous occasions. Once I arranged for him to listen to a book I had recorded. He spent some time listening but did not take up the option of reading the book for himself. However, by Week 5 there was some change: after I had spent some time reading a picture book with him, he read a fiction title, *Thing.* That was followed by a week's holiday with his family, and when he returned to school for the remaining weeks of term, his engagement with texts was restricted to short verse and picture books.

The first weeks of Term 2 were another settling-down period. He chose five books in the first week but finished none of them. In the second week, again with help over his selection, he finished one fiction text and spent two days listening to tapes. Over the next four weeks a new pattern began to emerge. He spent more time on one or two fiction and short story texts, although he did not complete them. Engagement was also evident with the non-fiction texts he chose.

One of the fiction texts he attempted at this time was being read to the whole class during Shared Reading. I knew that Dallas would have difficulty with the text, but I interpreted his response as an engagement cue — he was re-reading the chapters that had been read that morning and attempting to read on to find out what would happen.

During Weeks 7 and 8 something of a breakthrough occurred. He was encouraged to read a short story text suggested by another student who sat at his table cluster. His engagement with this text lasted for six days, and another two days were spent well engaged with non-fiction. Weeks 9 to 12 continued this pattern of engagement. Another fiction title was completed, although a more difficult one was returned to the shelves after two days. More engagement with works of non-fiction was also evident.

In Term 3 Dallas' pattern of choice favoured non-fiction. He was very much involved in research on gorillas and spent SSR reading text related to primates. He finished only two fiction titles during the term. He did attempt several others, but returned them to the shelves when he found them beyond his experience. However, these attempts did suggest a willingness to take on a title that interested him, even if it was beyond his reach. Another instance of this was when he chose the original, adult text of *Gorillas in the Mist,* from which I had read snippets to the whole class. I viewed his readiness to approximate and take risks as a sign of development.

Term 4 saw the pattern continue. Dallas would choose a text for himself and begin enthusiastically and in anticipation of finishing, but after three or four days he would return it unfinished. The texts were those he had seen others enjoy and share. Although I was uncertain about what meaning he constructed from the texts, I did not discourage his attempts. At the end of the year he still required support from teachers and others in choosing books, and I was left with the impression that he had not yet established what was within his range of reading experience.

DALLAS' SILENT READING RECORD

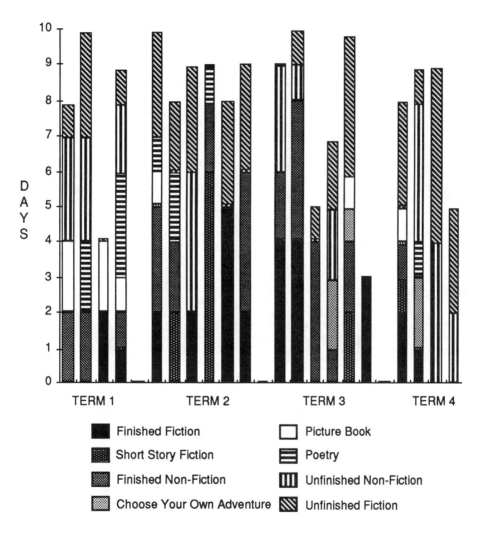

Dallas' pattern was repeated by other readers whose interest level lay well beyond their reading process experience. Knowing what they could read comfortably was, I realised, the first step in gaining control over their own reading and building towards the texts they wished to read. Becoming able to take on this responsibility, as many children did at various times in the year, was a major developmental step and one that Dallas had not yet managed.

3 Collaborative evaluation

JOSEPH	DALLAS
1.NUMBER OF BOOKS READ COMPLETELY: 14	1.NUMBER OF BOOKS READ COMPLETELY: 17
2.TYPES – FICTION: 2 NON-FICTION: 5 PICTURE BOOKS: 3 POETRY: 4	2.TYPES – FICTION: 2 NON-FICTION: 5 PICTURE BOOKS: 6 POETRY: 4
3.NUMBER OF BOOKS NOT COMPLETED: 2	3.NUMBER OF BOOKS NOT COMPLETED: 14
4.MOST FAVOURITE BOOK READ: Sister Madge's Book of Nuns (Poetry)	4.MOST FAVOURITE BOOK READ: Tailypo (Picture Book)
AUTHOR: Doug Macleod	AUTHOR: Joanne Galdone
5.WHY YOU ENJOYED IT: I liked it because of the comedy, the action and the rhymes.	5.WHY YOU ENJOYED IT: I like it because I took it home and read it to my brother.
6.COMMENTS ON MY READING PROGRESS: I think my reading progress is kind of good.	6.COMMENTS ON MY READING PROGRESS: My reading is o.k. but there is not many good books.
7.MY TEACHER'S COMMENTS: Joseph, I'm very pleased with your reading too. I would like you to try some fiction books for some variety. Get one you'll be really interested in – how about trying 'Deezle Boy', a story about a boy your age who is crazy about trains, especially diesel trains?	7.MY TEACHER'S COMMENTS: I'm pleased you enjoyed 'Tailypo'. I liked reading that with you. You should try to find books that suit you, Dallas; then you'll be able to sit longer and enjoy them. What about the new ones I've bought such as 'Hank Pank In Love'?

Reading evaluation sheets completed after ten weeks of school

Students used their own records to collate information for the reading evaluation sheet. This process involved them in reflecting on their reading patterns (and gave them a clear purpose for accurate record keeping). I overheard many comments that showed surprise at their own reading achievements.

The purpose of counting titles under certain categories was to show readers their pattern of choice. It was not important that one student had read twenty books and another ten. I made this clear by explaining that books differed in length and content, that readers read at different rates, and that some students liked to read at home as well as during SSR. I stressed that I was interested in the pattern — what particular types of text were read and how often texts were completed — and when I had digested the information the students gave me, I was able to make suggestions for their future reading choices.

Joseph's evaluation sheet responses reinforced my concern that he was not engaging often enough with the sort of narrative text that would involve him in unravelling plots, drawing inferences, making predictions and expanding his understanding of the complex language structures frequently found in fiction texts. He needed to engage with such models to enhance his command of English, which for him was a second language.

Towards the end of the year I decided to check my own evaluations against the students' perceptions of themselves. To do this, I asked them to complete a sheet of responses, circling those that best described them as readers. The list, drawn from the year's sum of observations, interactions and analysis, comprised the commonly occurring responses to the 'program activities', i.e. what the students did during SSR. The responses selected by Joseph and Dallas are shown below.

WHAT I DO WHEN I'M READING	
JOSEPH'S RESPONSE	DALLAS' RESPONSE
* Able to choose a book and finish it. (mostly)	* Have some difficulties choosing a book and finishing it.
* Can usually choose a book that I like.	* Take a long time to choose a book.
* Rarely ask the teacher to help me choose a book.	* Ask the teacher to help me choose a book.
* Can read without taking notice of visitors and other interruptions.	
* Remember what I was reading yesterday when I am asked.	* Remember what I was reading yesterday when I am asked.
* Choose the same type of book often.	* Choose the same type of book often.
* Find it hard not to talk to my neighbour during silent reading.	
* Like to make up my own mind about what to read.	
* Read books that other people have read.	* Read books that other people have read.
* Will stop reading a book after about one chapter if I don't like it.	* Will stop reading after two days if I don't like a book.
* Read about one book a week if it is long.	* Read about one book a week if it is long.
* Don't get up often in silent reading to change my book.	
* Don't finish books quickly – only read them here at school.	* Don't finish books quickly – only read them here at school.

* Rarely ask my neighbour or teacher to help me with something I don't understand.	* Ask my neighbour or teacher to help me when I get stuck on something.
* Enjoy the books I read.	* Enjoy the books I read.
* Take notice what others say about books but make up my own mind in the end.	* Read a book only if it was suggested by the teacher or my friends.
* After reading a long book that really took a lot of concentration, I choose a book or a magazine that is easier to read.	
	* When I come to a word I haven't seen before, I read on past it and guess its meaning, or don't worry about it if what I'm reading still makes sense. (sometimes)
* When I come to a word or a phrase I haven't seen before, I spend some time working it out, and if I can't, I stop reading and ask someone.	* When I come to a word or a phrase I haven't seen before, I spend some time working it out, and if I can't, I stop reading and ask someone. (sometimes)
* During the reading of a book I have to sometimes be encouraged to keep reading until I have finished .	* During the reading of a book I have to sometimes be encouraged to keep reading until I have finished. (sometimes)
* When choosing a book I like to find out from someone who has already read it if it's a good book. If the other person didn't like it, I don't read it.	* When choosing a book I like to find out from someone who has already read it if it's a good book. If the other person didn't like it, I don't read it.
* I don't have to find out what a book is about from someone else because I read the blurb and make up my own mind.	
* The cover doesn't make a big difference when I'm choosing a book.	* Make a decision whether to read a book by how interesting the cover looks. (sometimes)
* The size of the print isn't as important as what the book is about when I am making a choice.	* I check to see how small the print is before choosing a book.
* Like to tell others about exciting or interesting parts of the book after silent reading time.	
* Sometimes tell my mum or dad about a good book that I am reading.	* Sometimes tell my mum or dad about a good book that I am reading.
	* Usually don't talk about my books to my parents or the teacher.
* Often check to see how much I have to read before I complete the book.	
* Sometimes I am disappointed when a book ends because I wanted to know more about it.	* Sometimes I am disappointed when a book ends because I wanted to know more about it.
	* Prefer to read books that have some illustrations. (sometimes)

* Quite happy to read books with or without illustrations.	* Quite happy to read books with or without illustrations. (sometimes)
* I don't mind being asked by the teacher to read a part of my book to her.	
* Don't like to stop for a rest during silent reading.	* Don't like to stop for a rest during silent reading. (sometimes)
* Not concerned about having to finish quickly. Happy to take my time and enjoy a long book.	
* Reember what I was up to in my reading – don't usually read the same part again.	
* Make predictions in my head about what is going to happen further on in the book. Think about it after I have stopped reading.	

Joseph's and Dallas' responses were consistent with the evaluations I had made. Although the majority of Dallas' responses suggested non-engagement, there were some that pointed towards engagement. It was notable that while Joseph responded to one of almost all sets of descriptors, Dallas did not, and inferences can be drawn as much from the responses he did not select as from those he did. For example, he passed over the response indicating that he frequently changed his text in silent reading. Either he was unaware of this pattern, or else he considered that it was a normal thing for readers to do.

After analysing the responses, I was confident that the conclusions I had drawn about each student's language learning at the end of Year 5 were consistent with the student's own views. Each school report was a description of the combined realities of teacher and learner. The evaluations that I ultimately made of the learning outcomes of all the students were the result of a collaborative and responsive process.

Conclusion

By 'sitting beside' my students I had come to *know* them in ways that informed my beliefs and thus my practice. The recursive processes of responsive evaluation — responding to the things students do and how they do them within a learning context — enabled me and the students to make inferences about their knowledge, understanding, abilities and attitudes, and to use these inferences to extend their learning. The means of assessment provided the means for interaction, and my own expectations were continually mediated by the students' perceptions of their learning.

References

Goodman, Y., Watson, D. & Burke, C. 1987, *Reading Miscue Inventory: Alternative Procedures*, Owen, New York.

Hancock, J. 1991, The description analysis and evaluation of the process experienced by a teacher-researcher in implementing responsive evaluation as a mode of assessment of literacy development in a whole language classroom, MEd (Hons) thesis, University of Wollongong.

Rowntree, D. 1977, *Assessing Students: How Shall We Know Them?*, Harper and Row, London.

10 PARENTS AND ASSESSMENT

Ros Fryar, Nan Johnston & Jane Leaker

Over the past four years we have spent a considerable amount of time reviewing, changing and refining our classroom assessment practices. What triggered this activity was our involvement in a Graduate Diploma course in order to become LLIMY (Literacy and Learning in the Middle Years) tutors.

The course's intense focus on children's learning made us realise that neither they nor their parents had any real involvement in the assessment process. We also recognised that if our assessment practices were to have any real purpose and were to give the children some direction for their future learning, there needed to be a three-way communication between teacher, parent and child. By sharing our ideas and approaches we have developed practices, adaptable to any grade level, which enable this communication to take place. Our approach is not unique, however: many of our colleagues have successfully developed similar continuous assessment practices to meet their needs.

While this chapter outlines the major components of our present practice, we are still seeking new ideas and experimenting with them. None the less, given current trends in assessment in Australia (e.g. the introduction of attainment levels in South Australia this year), we are confident that we already have in place a set of practices which will easily enable us to meet the demands of determining attainment levels for each child in every curriculum area.

Communicating with parents

At the beginning of the year we establish communication with parents to let them know what are the expectations and purposes of our assessment practices and what their role in the process is. We do this in a variety of ways.

Questionnaire

In the first week of Term 1 a questionnaire is sent home to parents seeking their perceptions of their children's learning. The questions can be wide and varied, or just focus on a couple of curriculum areas such as reading and writing. Questions generally included are:

What are your child's main interests?

What do you feel are your child's strengths?

What do you feel are your child's weaknesses?

Are there any areas of your child's development that particularly concern you?

Is there anything you would like discussed in detail at the parent-teacher information evening early this term?

Most parents are very happy to fill in the questionnaire as they feel that the knowledge they have of their children is being valued by the teacher. The information they supply can often yield insights into how best to provide support for some children.

When questionnaires are sent home, it is important to state your purpose for wanting the information and to give parents the option of speaking to you personally rather than providing written answers. (This is often appreciated by parents for whom English is their second language.)

Parent-teacher information evening

An information evening for parents is usually held in the first few weeks of Term 1. This is when expectations for the year, curriculum areas, student behaviour, etc. are discussed. Most importantly, it is the time when we explain very clearly the beliefs about children's learning and language which are the basis of our classroom practice. At this stage the parents have already seen their children's assessment books (discussed below), which we send home once a week, beginning in Week 1. As a result we find we have little trouble in 'selling' our form of assessment, for parents can already see that they are receiving more information about their children's activities than ever before. The evening gives them an opportunity to find out why we have chosen this form of assessment and how we can work together to maximise their children's learning.

A written summary of what has been discussed during the evening is given to parents as they leave, so that they have a permanent copy to refer to as needed. The summary is also distributed to parents unable to attend.

Class newsletters and work samples

Regular newsletters are sent home to keep parents informed about classroom activities. They are usually written in conjunction with the children, who take turns in small groups to help produce them. They cover such things as topics of investigation in various curriculum areas, achievements, special occasions, things to remember, and invitations to class activities.

Assignments and examples of children's work from different curriculum areas are sent home regularly for parents to see and comment on if they wish. These work samples are kept in a portfolio, large scrap book or three-ringed binder. They help give a fuller picture of the children's development than the weekly visits of the assessment book could provide on their own. Positive and constructive written comments let parents know how their children are progressing, what their strengths are, and often what their next challenge is going to be.

The assessment book

The assessment book is a means of providing immediate feedback to students to enable them to improve their learning. It also provides an open, three-way communication system.

Before we began using assessment books, we kept anecdotal notes to use when speaking to parents at report time. The students kept their own records as well, including books they had read, pieces they had written, and so on. What has changed since then is our audience and the assessors. No longer are our notes for our eyes only, but for our students and their parents too. Students are playing an important role in assessing themselves; parents are being given specific information about their children's learning and management of tasks, and about the content of the curriculum. And since parents are now included in the assessment process, formal reports and/or interviews hold no surprises for them.

How best to store assessment information so that it is accessible and easy to manage is something that must be decided at the beginning. Your resources, what you want to include in the book and the ages of your students will all affect what you use. Two of us, Jane and Ros, use a 96-page exercise book, divided into sections, for each of our students. Nan, on the other hand, photocopies the various sections onto different coloured paper and holds them together with spiral binding. These books will probably become the most heavily used documents in the class, and so they need to be strong enough to survive daily handling as well as being taken home regularly.

With experience, we have developed a series of sections in which information is recorded. They are described in some detail below, but, broadly, Section 1 tells students and parents what the book is for and how to use it. Sections 2, 3 and 4 provide opportunities for students to reflect on their learning, reveal their anxieties, celebrate their successes and ask for the help they need. These sections also provide parents with information about the day-to-day life of their children at school. Sections 5-11 contain information about student learning in each of the required areas of study outlined by the Education Department of South Australia (1990). Section 12 is a place for students to practice planning their time.

1 A letter to the students and parents

> The Assessment folder is a very important source of information for your assessment.   It will be used to help write school reports and to keep your parents informed about what you are doing and how you are coping with your school work and your learning.
>
>   It is a place for you to plan your work, reflect on your learning, think about what you can do to help yourself and keep records of your achievements.
>
>   You will need to maintain this booklet, keep it up to date and take it home each week for your parents to read, make comments and sign.
>
>   If you have any problems you can talk to me about it and I will help you.
>   Good luck.
>
>   Mrs J.

2 Goal setting for the term

At the beginning of each term we demonstrate how we set goals for ourselves and for the class as a whole. Then the students are asked to set their own. In the first term this involves goals for each curriculum area and some general goals. However, as the students become more familiar with goal setting during the year, they decide how to organise this section and what to include in it. At the end of each term they look back and reflect, evaluating their achievements in relation to their goals. There is space for both teacher and parent to comment on the student's self-evaluation.

3 Weekly reviews

There is further opportunity for students to write reflectively in the weekly review, which is described at the end of this chapter. We have chosen to discuss this section more fully as we believe that weekly reviews are particularly suited to opening communication channels between teacher, student and parent.

   If you are going to embark on a similar process of assessment, this is a good place to start. We all began our assessment books with this idea, and the sense of excitement it generated in all concerned was more than enough to encourage us to develop other forms of assessment.

4 Term review

Students are encouraged to think back over the whole term by referring to their weekly reviews, assignments, workbooks and record keeping, and then to write about what they enjoyed, what has been useful to them, what improvements or changes they would like to make, what opinions they have about their behaviour, and anything else they wish to comment on. There is also a place for parents to comment.

5 English language

This section is broken into four sub-sections.

Reading

At the beginning of the reading section the students reflect on themselves as readers. They do so at the beginning of the year (which helps us find out about each student), and again in the middle of the year (to see if any changes have occurred). The information gathered helps us to make specific plans to help them develop as readers, and also shows whether they are able and/or willing to set specific goals for themselves.

Confessions of a Reader

Write about
- what you think about yourself as a reader
- what kinds of books you enjoy and why
- what kinds of books you find difficult and why
- what challenges you could set yourself in reading this year
- what help you need to achieve them
- what you will need to do to achieve them

Students are also expected to keep a dated record of the books they read, with a rating and brief comment. This record is used to track a number of things: emergent reading patterns, whether there is a range of reading, what books are not completed, purposes for reading, and the number of books read over a particular period. At intervals the record is discussed between student and teacher.

Conference notes are kept too. Parent helpers, teacher and peers summarise what was discussed. There may be a specific focus for the conference (e.g. discuss plot, mood, characters or setting), or it may be open-ended, allowing the student to decide the topic of discussion.

Reading Conference   *Name:*

Title and Author:

Summary:

                                    Signed: *date:*

Focused observations make up the final part of the reading section and are written by the teacher. These observations may refer to·

- the reading behaviours and strategies used by the students (e.g. finger pointing, using picture cues, re-reading, correcting)

- concepts (uses of reading, reading processes)

- attitudes (choosing to read, self-selecting)

- responses to fiction (identifying main characters, commenting on plot)

- responses to non-fiction (skim reading, taking notes).

The observations are easily recorded on an A4 sheet ruled to a grid, which can then be cut up and pasted into individual assessment books.

Writing

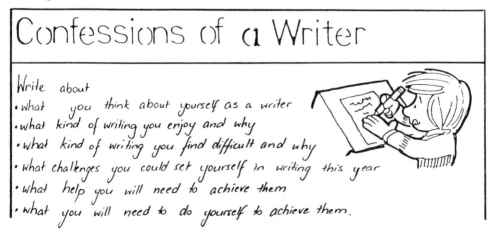

Confessions of a Writer

Write about
- what you think about yourself as a writer
- what kind of writing you enjoy and why
- what kind of writing you find difficult and why
- what challenges you could set yourself in writing this year
- what help you will need to achieve them
- what you will need to do yourself to achieve them.

As in reading, the writing section begins with a space for self-reflection. This is followed by a chart for the students to record what writing they have done. It is divided into columns with these headings:

Title	Form	Audience	Drafting started finished	Proofread by me and ...	Publish yes no

Conference notes for writing differ from those for reading in that the student always sets the topic for discussion.

Writing Conference   Name:

Title:
I want to talk about:

Suggestions:

                                Signed: date:

We also use focused observations to look at:

- concepts (cultural/social influences, audience)

- attitudes (commitment, willingness to change)

- strategies (pre-writing, writing, post-writing)

- aspects of written products (ideas and information, organisation, language, mechanics).

As with reading, these focused observations are based on *Literacy Assessment in Practice* (Badger et al. 1991).

Word study

Students share their views of themselves as spellers in 'Confessions of a Speller'. Questions like *What do you do when you come to a word you don't know?* provide us with a wonderful insight into their understanding of a number of spelling strategies. And by focusing them on such questions as *Are you a good speller? How do you know? Who do you know that's a good speller? What makes him or her a good speller?*, we also gain an insight into their self-concept and how they measure themselves.

Each of us believes that children best learn to spell in the context of writing, and so the students work on negotiated assignments which cover a wide range of reading and writing tasks. They are expected to complete the writing process of drafting, revising, re-drafting and publishing in all parts of these assignments. They are assessed on each part and have their own opportunity to comment on the assignment. Parents are also invited to comment when the assignment goes home.

Oral communication

This part of the assessment book consists of focused observations from the teacher, peers and the student, based on specific objectives. For example, prior to a prepared talk, students may be told that they need to focus on three things (e.g. eye contact with the audience, use of prompt cards and loudness of voice), which will then be used as the basis of assessment.

Sections 6-11

The next six sections deal with other areas of the curriculum, namely: mathematics, society and environment, science and technology, health and personal development, and the arts. Assessment follows patterns similar to those described for earlier sections and includes students' own reflections, the teacher's observations and comments and parents' comments. However, the final section (12) is common to all curriculum areas.

12 Assignments

Students in our classes are often involved in working on negotiated assignments, which gives them opportunities to organise their own work. They are encouraged to plan their work and to place tasks on a time line. This helps them to be realistic about their goals, to keep up-to-date with their tasks, to negotiate extensions of time when necessary and plan their home work. It provides parents with the same information, and we find this section particularly useful as a focus for parent-teacher interviews, as well as for student-teacher discussions.

Some hints

We have gone through a lot of trial and error to evolve our system. We found that discussing what we each thought was important to include helped to firm up our ideas, but it certainly did not happen all at once. We took risks in handing over a good portion of assessment to students and parents. However,

we have all found that it really works as a way of providing ongoing information about student performance and involvement to those most concerned:
students, parents and teachers.

Our experience enables us to offer the following hints for starting and using
an assessment book.

- Choose an area of curriculum with which you feel comfortable.

- Use the book every day and take class time to establish routines for using
it.

- Demonstrate the kinds of writing involved. Remember that students may
not have experienced them before.

- Reteach the use of the book when necessary.

- Always respond and be positive in your responses.

- Explain to the students why you are using the book (they are the main
audience).

- Keep the language simple, meaningful and explicit.

- Develop and use your recording systems according to your objectives.

- Find someone to work with to develop an assessment book.

- Start small — do not try it all at once.

- Don't be discouraged by minor setbacks. Establishing an assessment book
is a long process. Keep going; it really is worth it.

- Be adaptable. Assessment books can be evolved from your beliefs and
your current practices and record keeping.

- Be open with parents. Explain what you are doing and why. You might
talk about your uncertainties and reservations: e.g. your handwriting may
not be as clear as usual because you are trying to give immediate response; you are writing 'off the top of your head' and so there may well be
some errors.

- Provide lots of opportunities for all parties to be involved in assessment. It
does not all rest on your shoulders.

Weekly reviews

As we have indicated, an important component of assessment in our classes is the weekly review, in which students reflect on their week's work, attitude and behaviour. It also gives them an opportunity to set goals for the next week.

When students have finished writing, we add our reflective remarks. The reviews are then put into their assessment books and taken home for parents to read, sign and comment on.

While the weekly review works well at all levels, the format will vary according to the age of your students, their experience with self-assessment, and your knowledge of their abilities and experiences. We have found that once our students become experienced with writing reviews, we are able to negotiate a variety of formats for use throughout the year. By providing a variety of formats you are able to maintain their enthusiasm, respond to varying needs and improve your program planning.

A weekly review may contain any of the following items.

- A blank page inviting your students to respond to their week's learning.

- Focused questions, e.g:
  What do you feel you have learned/achieved this week?
  What things did you do in class this week that helped you learn?
  In what areas do you feel you need more help or practice?
  What activity did you find most enjoyable and why?

- Rating along a continuum:

  poor 0———1———2———3———4———5 excellent

  – this week overall
  – yard behaviour
  – class behaviour
  – curriculum subjects.

  We also ask students to explain why they decided on each particular rating.

- Goal setting:

My goals next week.	How will I achieve them?	How will I know I've succeeded?
1.		
2.		
3.		

- Teacher comment.

- Parent comment.

One difficulty that many students have is recalling everything they did during the week. To help overcome this, we have used the following strategies prior to writing:

- brainstorming the week's activities

- enlarging and pinning up a copy of the teacher's program for all to read

- maintaining an ongoing list of each day's activities.

Each of these helps students to recall what the highlights have been for them and ensures a range of responses for us to read.

Initially we demonstrate how to write weekly reviews, emphasising as we do so our expectation that students will write about their own learning. We find that some students new to this kind of writing use our model until they gain the confidence to vary it. We also demonstrate goal setting, which is important because many students tend to set broad goals (e.g. *improve my handwriting*) rather than specific goals (e.g. *improve how I join the* r *and* o *together*).

For students, the most valuable part of the review is the teacher's response. Our method is to provide immediate and relevant feedback. It shows the students that we value their learning, their efforts and their development. Our responses acknowledge these things positively and indicate how we will help the student in the following week.

For the teacher, it is a time-consuming job. It may take two hours to respond to the whole class when you first start, but as you gain experience in responding this time shortens considerably. The rewards are great if you persevere. Your responses are eagerly awaited and you gain more detailed knowledge of your students' strengths and weaknesses, their preferred learning styles, their perceptions of class life, and the tasks in which they have been involved. With such knowledge you are able to better plan effective learning for all students.

For parents, the weekly review provides real knowledge about their children's activities at school, the progress they are making, the feelings they have about their work, and how they can be helped at home. Weekly reviews have an immediacy for parents. There is no longer any 'hidden curriculum' because they are aware of your expectations of the children. The positive nature of your feedback encourages a feeling of approachability, and allows parents to follow up any issues, problems and concerns they may have, promptly.

We have noticed that since we have been using weekly reviews in our classes, very few parents request comparisons between students, marks or grades. Neither students nor parents are using these as a measure of students' progress. Instead parents listen to their children and share the ongoing self and teacher evaluation which they receive weekly. Informal interviews between teacher and parents are often initiated by parents. Because of our shared understanding of the children's learning, attitudes and development, we are usually able to reach a mutually satisfying resolution to most problems.

Conclusion

Many schools have a policy that requires formal parent-teacher interviews. We find that preparing for these is no longer an onerous task. With the assessment book parents already have a sound knowledge of what has been taught, what is expected and what has been achieved, and they are able to talk about specific areas of concern rather than generalities.

While we do not believe that formal written reports are necessary if ongoing assessment is in place, some schools still require them. You will find that the assessment that you and your students have been involved in will make this a simple task. It is our experience that the more teachers use ongoing assessment and reporting which is shared with parents and involves student self-assessment, the more parents request this kind of assessment to replace formal school reporting.

References

Badger, L., Dilena, M., Peters, J., Webster, C. & Weeks, B. 1991, *Literacy Assessment in Practice: R–7 Language Arts,* Education Department of South Australia, Adelaide.

Education Department of South Australia 1990, *Educating for the 21st Century: A Charter for Public Schooling in South Australia,* Adelaide.

Leaker, J. 1991, *Windows on Practice: Student Assessment Using Work Assessment Books,* Education Department of South Australia, Adelaide.

Weeks, B. & Leaker, J. 1991, *Managing Literacy Assessment with Young Learners,* Era Publications, Adelaide.

11 DEVELOPING A MULTIDIMENSIONAL INTERACTIVE INFORMATION NETWORK

Heather Fehring

For a long time I have questioned the assumption that an education system needs to impose state-wide testing to demonstrate accountability to the public. If the public requires demonstration of literacy standards, why is the solution to impose literacy measures designed at the bureaucratic centre of the system — in other words, a top-down model of measurement? Why have we not looked for a bottom-up model with greater conviction?

Historically, we have tended to collect quantitative data about a student's performance, often relying on externally devised measures and sometimes following central directives. For example, Chris had a percentile rank of 75 on this spelling test; Peta was in stanine 5 on that writing test; the average Year 6 student would achieve a 'reading age' of 11 years 5 months on this reading test. However, it is now widely accepted that school policy, curriculum practice and assessment strategies should be integrally tied together, so that each flows consistently from the other, as shown below.

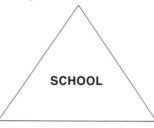

School Policy
philosophical and educational
principles underlying the
organisation of the school

SCHOOL

**Curriculum
Practice**

learning experiences
which embody the beliefs
expressed
in the school policy

**Assessment
Strategies**

techniques which reflect
the principles
stated in the school policy
and the reality of the school's
curriculum practice

Running record
A systematic technique for observing, recording and analysing students' oral reading behaviour. It is used in the Early Literacy In-Service Course (ELIC).

Miscue analysis
A technique for recording and analysing students' oral reading errors in order to gain an insight into the reading processes they employ.

Cloze procedure
Involves getting students to fill in words deliberately omitted from a passage of text. When well designed, it allows teachers to analyse the silent reading strategies that students are using.

Retelling procedures
Various techniques which demonstrate students' understanding of a text. They are best described in *Read and Retell* (Brown & Cambourne 1987).

Proofread-check-correct procedure
A method which encourages a student to proofread a passage to identify possible errors, check them against a writing resource (e.g. a dictionary or wall chart), and correct any inaccuracies.

Anecdotal/observational records
Logbooks/journals/notebooks in which a teacher records observations of students' behaviour in the classroom.

Self-assessment journals
Journals kept by students to reflect on their own progress in particular curriculum areas.

Self-evaluation statements
Critical commentaries by students about their own learning processes.

Reading choice records
Many teachers require students to maintain some form of reading log, which can then be used to survey and discuss patterns of book selection and reading.

Writing portfolios/folios
These folders contain representative samples (i.e. draft, edited and published versions) of different types of writing. They include work from different points in time to record and demonstrate longitudinal progress.

Qualitative assessment procedures

Accordingly, over the last decade or so, there has been a move by school communities away from a reliance upon quantitative assessment measures, particularly standardised reading, writing and spelling tests, to qualitative or descriptive strategies. Such strategies are classroom-based and are often designed by the class teacher. They aim to describe what literacy understandings and behaviours each child exhibits in authentic situations which reflect the normal day-to-day reading and writing tasks of the classroom. This kind of assessment is felt to be more effective in meeting the needs of students, teachers and parents.

We now have at our disposal numerous techniques providing a variety of information on which we can draw to understand a student's language progress. These techniques, a selection of which is set out on the facing page, allow us to provide rich, qualitative data at the local school level.

However, many teachers have experienced problems in developing their own assessment tools. It takes time to develop and implement a classroom-based strategy effectively, whether it be a retelling protocol or a miscue analysis, and time is always short. In addition, some teachers feel the need of more professional development. What we need to do now is to investigate how to maximise the qualitative components of classroom-based techniques, share the accumulated expertise of local schools and minimise time-consuming mechanical processing, while acknowledging that systems need information for administrative decision making.

I propose that we investigate the possibility of developing a multidimensional interactive information network. A student's language profile should consist of a variety of sources of information (multidimensional knowledge). A network could connect users (e.g. teachers, schools, etc.) by utilising a variety of communication mechanisms (e.g. personal computers, fax, video conferencing, video phones, scanners). Not only would such a network allow users to have a 'dialogue' (interact) about particular students' abilities; it would also facilitate the exchange of ideas and assessment techniques (information network).

It is possible, even with current personal computer (PC) technology, to create local area networks (LANs). A local area network is simply a number of computers (e.g. PCs, printers, etc.) which are electronically connected to each other to exchange and process information. The word 'local' signifies that the network is geographically small — as, for example, between individual classrooms or departments within a school. The diagram overleaf shows one such LAN.

Teacher 1 (Pat, in a Year 4 class) has developed an interesting series of cloze passages as part of the class assessment procedure for a social education topic on change which is being studied in the upper school. Teacher 4 (Morgan, in a composite Year 5/6 class) has developed a very effective self-assessment schedule for spelling. Pat and Morgan can exchange practices via their internal school-based LAN.

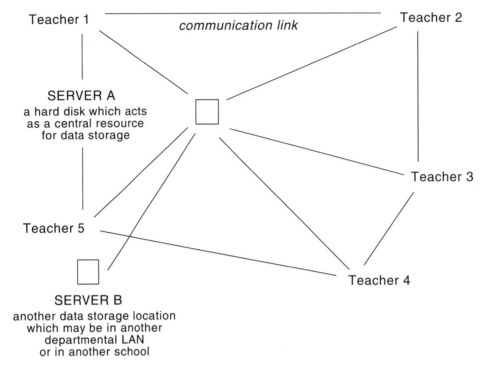

A local area network (LAN)

It is also possible to set up wide area networks (WANs). A wide area network is simply a computer network extending over a large geographic area. It may be made up of several LANs. For example, within a region or state, many individual school-based LANs could be connected to each other, allowing different schools to exchange information. The diagram opposite shows how one such WAN might operate.

School A has developed a series of criterion-based learning contracts for a Year 7 to 9 English course, and School B is using the same English curriculum guidelines. School A can share and transfer assessment practices to School B. A WAN could be especially beneficial for small rural schools or remote schools unable to get easy access to specialists. For example, School C has an experienced ELIC tutor on staff. School D, an isolated school, could fax or electronically mail a particular student's assessment folio to this tutor. Via a WAN connection a two-way (tutor in School C – teacher in School D), or even a three-way (tutor in School C – teacher and student in School D) on-line consultation could take place. School E could utilise School D's miscue analysis procedure and processing capability to receive an (almost) instantaneous analysis of a student's strengths and an 'areas in need of further work' report. New ideas and techniques could be shared via an on-line 'assessment update bulletin'.

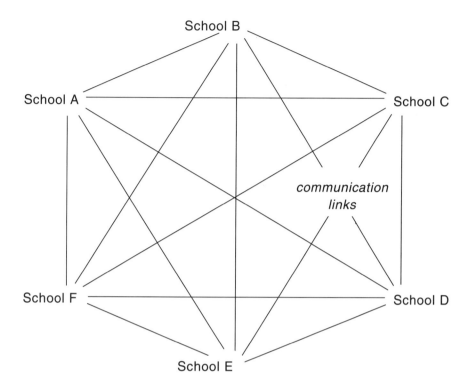

A wide area network (WAN)

By utilising WANs, schools could tap into locally constructed assessment procedures, still maintaining the integrity of the Policy – Curriculum Practice – Assessment Strategies principle outlined at the beginning of this chapter. Such a system could be a true bottom-up assessment model and displace top-down models.

As I have suggested, networks would also lend themselves to personal, interactive assessment practices, instead of the static, one-way, limited-time, paper and pencil techniques now current. A teacher, a student and a consultant could have live interaction via their respective PCs, faxes and phones. A 'discussion' could take place about the student's understanding of the proofreading and editing process in writing, or the practice of Look-Say-Cover-Write-Check in spelling, or about the student's reflections in response to a self-appraisal questionnaire on writing skills. On-line interactive assessment could be efficient and cost-effective in terms of travel and time saved, the utilisation of scarce expert personnel (e.g. psychologists, ELIC tutors), and well-constructed material.

It would also be possible to accumulate common components in a data bank at a district, regional or state level. The information could then be used at a system level to address such issues as allocation of funds, accountability and qualitative statements about literacy. This process would reflect the reality of classroom practice, and would be based on formative (ongoing) assessment rather than the summative variety characteristic of present notions of state-wide testing.

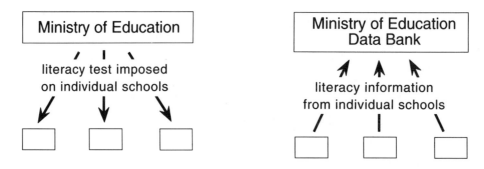

Top-down model of measurement   Bottom-up model of measurement

To develop a multidimensional interactive information network, we need to investigate the possibilities thoroughly now, and be trialling prototypes in the 1990s in preparation for the 21st century.

References

Brown, H. & Cambourne, B. 1987, *Read and Retell*, Methuen, Sydney. Distributed by Heinemann